LEADING IN THE AGE OF DIGITAL DISRUPTION

Building Resilient, High-Performing Teams in a Rapidly Changing World

MIKE PETERSON

No part of this publication may be reproduced, distributed, or transmitted in any form or by any means, including photocopying, recording, or other electronic or mechanical methods, without the prior written permission of the publisher, except in the case of brief quotations embodied in critical reviews and certain other noncommercial uses permitted by copyright law.

Limit of Liability/Disclaimer of Warranty: The publisher and author make no representations or warranties with respect to the accuracy or completeness of the contents of this book and specifically disclaim any implied warranties of merchantability or fitness for a particular purpose. The advice, strategies, and practices contained herein may not be suitable for every situation. Neither the publisher nor the author shall be liable for any damages arising from the use or misuse of the information provided in this book.

Any websites referenced in this book are provided for informational purposes only and do not constitute an endorsement. The publisher has no control over the content of these websites and assumes no responsibility for them or their availability.

The reader is encouraged to seek professional advice tailored to their individual circumstances.

This is a work of fiction. While efforts have been made to ensure accuracy, the names, characters, businesses, places, events, and incidents are either the product of the author's imagination or used in a fictitious manner. Any resemblance to actual persons, living or dead, or actual events is purely coincidental.

Cover design and interior formatting by KUHN Design Group | kuhndesigngroup.com

Copyright © 2025 by Apex Consulting Partners, LLC
All rights reserved.

ISBN: 979-8-9923170-0-8 (paperback)
ISBN: 979-8-9923170-1-5 (hardcover)
ISBN: 979-8-9923170-2-2 (eBook)

Published by Apex Publishing
Printed in the United States of America

First Edition: April 2025

For more resources and additional tools, visit https://www.apexconsulting.partners/.

This book is for those who aspire to lead with purpose, inspire others, and make a difference beyond titles and accolades. It is for the dreamers, the doers, and the changemakers. May it serve as both a guide and a reminder that true leadership leaves a legacy—not in achievements alone, but in the lives it touches along the way.

CONTENTS

Foreword 7

PART ONE: THE BRIGHTPATH STORY

A Company in Crisis 17

Monday 25

Setting Priorities 35

What We Permit 43

Shifting the Culture 49

The Finance Story 59

The R&D Story 67

The Executive Team 73

Emerging Resistance 77

The Brightpath Town Hall 83

Reconnecting with the Board Chair 89

Leadership Training 95

Client Outreach 101

The Quality Crisis 107

High Performance 113

The Burnout Leader 119

The Ultimatum 123

The Marketing Story 129

Marketing Between Leaders 135

Recruiting for the New Culture 141
The New Leader Arrives 147
Project Align 153
The Four-Fifty Crisis 159
Building a Next-Generation Company 171

PART TWO: LEADERSHIP THEORY AND PRACTICAL APPLICATION

Introducing Part Two 179
Building Trust as the Foundation of Leadership 183
Transparent Communication 193
Accountability Built on Trust 203
Servant Leadership: Leading by Serving Others 211
Leading Through Crisis 219
Fostering Innovation Through Leadership 227
Navigating Difficult Decisions 235
Practical Strategies for Leading Hybrid Teams 243
Conclusion 251

Your Leadership Journey 251
Tools and Resources 259
Acknowledgments 265
About the Author 267
About Apex Consulting Partners 269

FOREWORD

Over the years, I've had the privilege of practicing human resources (HR) and information technology (IT) in seventeen countries, working with thousands of leaders and their teams from all around the world. This global experience has shown me that while leadership principles are universal, their application varies depending on context and culture.

Along the way, I've read many books on leadership. While most of these books are inspiring and full of interesting theories and examples, I have noticed a common pattern. They often leave managers uncertain about how to translate those ideas into action.

Based on the gaps I've noticed in leadership books that lack actionable steps managers can take to implement great ideas, I felt the need to create a way to share what I've learned in my international career.

This is the book I wish I had when I started out—one with helpful tips and ideas that are clear, practical, and easy to implement.

Leadership may be complex, but understanding how to lead

doesn't have to be. Whether you're managing your first team or navigating the challenges of leading a global organization, this book is your leadership toolkit. It is a guide to flexible skills for solving problems and managing people. You'll get tools and build skills you can call upon to meet the unique needs of your team or organization in any situation.

I hope this book helps you navigate challenges with clarity and empowers you to inspire and guide others.

Leading in the Age of Digital Disruption is also designed to help you master the challenges of leadership in the digital age. The wide-ranging internet and the advent of artificial intelligence (AI), global teams, remote work, and hybrid models of participation have changed what it means to lead. There are new levels of flexibility, innovation, and diversity, along with new complexities: communication gaps, misaligned expectations, and the constant pressure to maintain culture and cohesion in an ever-broadening landscape.

To lead in the digital age, you must go beyond managing projects or hitting targets. You need to create a foundation of trust, foster clear and transparent communication, and hold yourself and your team accountable to accomplish shared goals. You must navigate the unique dynamics of modern work environments, where employees might be sitting in the same room, logging in from their home office, or collaborating from halfway across the globe. As you master these essential skills, you can unlock your team's true potential and position yourself and your organization to succeed.

To help you tackle these challenges head-on, I've included fictionalized scenarios I've experienced firsthand at many companies where I've worked—either as an executive or as a senior consultant.

This book explores its concepts through two lenses:

1. THE STORY OF A NEW CEO

In the first half, you'll follow Ethan, the newly appointed chief executive officer (CEO) of Brightpath Solutions, a fast-growing global tech company specializing in cutting-edge enterprise software solutions for global clients. It also provides staff augmentation in highly technical areas. The flagship offering, also called Brightpath, is a combined software and consultation system sold through subscriptions. Brightpath has about 750 employees in nine countries. Incorporated in Dublin, it has major offices in San Francisco, Washington, DC, Bangalore, London, Barcelona, Bangkok, Tallinn, and most recently, a branch has been added in Lagos.

Ethan steps into his new leadership role at a pivotal moment, replacing Victor, the original founder and CEO who had instigated the firm's signature technology five years earlier and brought Brightpath to prominence. Victor's fierce, numbers-driven approach prioritized performance over people, resulting in burnout, disengagement, and a fractured culture. It also led him and some of his top leaders to skate close to the edge at times, manipulating the numbers to make the company's revenue growth and ROI seem more favorable than they actually were.

While Brightpath teeters on the brink of scandal, high turnover and cultural strain have also left it dangerously close to failure. Ethan must pull his executive team together, rescue the company from impending disaster, and rebuild its foundation to ensure sustainable success.

2. THE LEADERSHIP PLAYBOOK

The second half of this book delves deeply into the leadership principles illustrated through Ethan's journey. I've included a comprehensive toolkit to support your efforts to lead effectively in any environment. You'll explore actionable strategies for fostering trust, practicing servant leadership, and leveraging emotional intelligence to inspire and empower your team. With a strong emphasis on trust, transparent communication, accountability, and navigating the complexities of hybrid and global workforces, this section provides the clarity needed to face real-world challenges.

It is important to recognize the pivotal role IT plays in driving success within hybrid environments. Reliable communication platforms, secure infrastructure, and effective collaboration tools serve as the backbone of global teams and hybrid workflows. Leaders must prioritize adaptive and robust IT strategies that align with their teams' needs, enabling a seamless integration of people and technology to foster innovation, productivity, and cohesion in today's dynamic workplace. That said, this book focuses solely on the human aspects of leadership, leaving the technical elements of IT outside its scope.

WHY THE QUALITY OF LEADERSHIP MATTERS

When you are given the title of leader and put in charge of a project, a team, a business, or a large company—it feels heady. You have the power to make things happen. You soon come to terms with the realities, however. At times of rapid change, leadership requires more than just a title. It requires the kind of skills that go with being accountable for results, getting people to work with you and make commitments, and organizing the flow of human activity.

Most leaders realize they don't have all the necessary skills. So, they ask for help with leadership. Typically, they want a magic bullet.

They may not phrase it that way, but when they talk about solutions and best practices, they're clearly asking: "How can I and my group operate with the most certainty of success?"

As a consultant on HR and IT issues, I am continually asked some variation of this question. Leaders recognize that their intuitive sense of what to do won't take them where they want to go. They have the sense that there are formulas to follow. If they just look hard enough, or ask the right expert, they will find the best practices they need.

It's a reasonable idea. And it's partly correct.

During the past fifty years, some basic skills have emerged for managing people in the digital age. There may not be a single magic bullet in management—that is, a set of practices applicable to all business situations—but there are better ways of doing things. These more effective management practices will generally get you closer to creating a highly productive, highly successful team or company.

Most of these practices involve a better understanding of people, leaders, and other decision-makers throughout the enterprise. A human-oriented leadership style recognizes how important people are to the success of the enterprise. After all, every company has access to the internet, AI, and other advanced technologies. Many have access to capital and resources. Those are almost essential commodities. But nobody has access to your people and your working relationship with them.

The skills required for human-oriented leadership involve building trust—which means establishing confidence in one another's reliability, integrity, intentions, and basic competence. You also need to create an environment of transparent communications, where everyone understands how their work fits into the greater whole and where people feel safe expressing their opinions, voicing concerns, and offering ideas. You must also foster accountability so that people can learn from both their errors and their successes, and practice servant leadership, where you put the needs of your team ahead of your own power and privilege.

Other factors are also important. You need to set priorities so that people are working on the challenges that make the greatest difference, navigate difficult decisions and crises, delegate authority effectively, and manage your own time so that you can effectively keep everyone going and remain at your best. All this has to happen in addition to managing the technical and professional aspects of the work.

The rationale for a human-oriented leadership style has increased significantly because of the added challenges of the hybrid work model. Even as companies return to the office, many employees continue to work remotely, and global teams are more common than ever. Leaders must adapt to this reality, finding new ways to connect, engage, and inspire their teams.

Other changes in the workplace involve the expanding use of AI and the increased productivity that goes with it. Some jobs are being rendered obsolete or replaced by AI, while some new jobs are just beginning to emerge. Add to this the increasingly global composition of many teams, the demographic shifts that place many younger employees in Asia, Africa, or central Europe, and the wide mix of attitudes and policies about diversity, equity, and inclusion, and you have an unprecedented range of pressures on leadership. Traditional rules and formulas for success won't cut it in today's world.

Many leaders get promoted because they have been recognized as outstanding individual contributors. Once they're in a leadership position, they're supposed to help others succeed. However, they often still spend 80 percent or more of their time as individual contributors.

This becomes a self-fulfilling prophecy. New leaders feel they have more ground to cover, so they don't have as much time to accomplish their own work—therefore, they have less time to spend on leading their team. As a result, they don't have time to develop themselves as leaders or to develop others to take on the responsibilities they once handled as individual contributors.

This is the challenge in a nutshell and the reason why many leaders are compelled to attend training seminars and read books on leadership. Once you are in this cycle, it is hard to break. If you want the highest probability of success for your business on a consistent basis, that requires you to continually increase your skills and the skills of others. You will have to lead by example, serve your team, and build a culture where trust, accountability, and communication are the foundation of success.

I invite you to read on and join Ethan as he navigates these issues and complexities. By the end of this journey, you'll not only have a deeper understanding of what it takes to lead in the digital age, but you'll also have the tools and insights to apply these lessons to your own leadership journey.

PART ONE

THE BRIGHTPATH STORY

A COMPANY IN CRISIS

Brightpath Solutions was a company on the rise—but also on the brink of collapse. It was a fast-growing, medium-sized tech firm with 750 employees in nine countries and an especially strong presence in the US and India. It specialized in cutting-edge software solutions tailored for its global clients based on its own Brightpath collection of interrelated digital platforms and AI models.

Victor, the founder and CEO, had started the company right out of graduate school. Under his leadership, Brightpath developed its first innovative app—and a culture focused solely on performance metrics and bottom-line results. As its customer base grew, Brightpath built up a fully remote product development team spread across the globe. This global structure offered access to top-tier talent. It also created challenges, including silos, communication gaps, and a growing divide between in-office and remote employees.

To its credit, Brightpath embraced a hybrid workplace model, with most team meetings taking place on video channels and a lot of operational support for collaboration across borders and time zones. Victor had understood from the start that he could attract top talent worldwide by offering flexibility and a chance to work with high performers wherever they were located. Brightpath occasionally flew its leading tech talent to conferences to meet face-to-face, but most of their interactions took place online. Many employees worked from home, especially in the US and Europe. This approach allowed the company to scale rapidly, growing from a small startup to a major player in the tech solutions industry in just five years.

While growth brought significant opportunities, it also introduced critical challenges. Victor often dismissed employee feedback and implemented sweeping policy changes without consulting anyone except Jennifer, the chief financial officer (CFO). They were both prone to micromanaging others, and over time, their rigid, numbers-driven approach created a high-pressure environment where managers were pushed to their limits, often at the expense of their personal lives. Long hours, sleepless nights, and constant stress became the norm.

As the company grew, it kept burning through capital. There were three funding rounds in the first five years, which raised the pressure for expansion. Burnout and disengagement spread throughout the organization after the fourth year, driving some high-performing employees to leave while others struggled to remain motivated. Brightpath's once collaborative and innovative culture eroded under the weight of unrelenting demands.

Then came a critical challenge. Several large clients terminated their contracts in the same quarter, saying they weren't getting the support they expected. Staff turnover levels reached a crisis point, leaving many teams severely understaffed and falling behind. An audit of R&D funds showed that Victor and Jennifer had quietly moved money to reinforce projects they had publicly agreed to shut down.

Recognizing the cracks within the organization, the Board of Directors moved rapidly to force Victor and Jennifer out of the company. The chairman of the board, a well-known venture capitalist named Tanya Grayson, had taken personal responsibility for this action. Without a change in leadership, she feared the company's future was at risk.

Grayson had grown up in Palo Alto and taken a job out of Stanford at a Sand Hill Road venture fund. She had shown a knack for managing a few strategic investments back in the early 1990s, had weathered the fallout when the dot-com bubble burst, and had gone on to promote some business-process-app unicorns at early stages. Her mother had moved to the US from Mumbai, and she had taken advantage of her Indian contacts to make some early investments there, which had also paid off. About ten years earlier, now at her own firm, she had pulled together the first two rounds of funding for Brightpath. She had always been Victor's advocate until about a year before, when she had visibly retreated from supporting him—an early sign that he was overreaching. She had a reputation as an empathetic venture capitalist, one of the few who understood the relationship between quality leadership and successful results.

Now, after evaluating several external candidates, Grayson realized the solution was already within the company. Ethan Caldwell, Brightpath's chief human resources officer (CHRO), had consistently argued for sustainable growth based on talent development and investment. Known for his collaborative leadership style, focus on trust, and commitment to accountability, Ethan emerged as the ideal candidate to lead the company through this critical transition.

Grayson and the other board members recognized that it was unusual to promote a human resources executive to the top slot in the company. However, they also had experience with outside turnaround artists coming in, and she, as much as anyone, understood that even in tech companies, the human factor made all the difference. If Ethan could pull Brightpath out of its slump, Grayson thought, then he could be establishing a model for corporate strategy that could be widely influential among their holdings. Maybe the appointment of CHRO to CEO would become a new management fad.

The removal of Victor and Jennifer was kept intensely quiet. One week in April, they both went on vacation, and never returned to the office. That Wednesday afternoon, Tanya Grayson asked Ethan to meet her for an early dinner at the Capital Grille. They sat there talking until almost midnight.

They had barely placed their drink orders when Tanya leaned forward. She was a trim Indian American woman in her early 60s, which made her seem almost grandmotherly to Ethan. At the same time, her presence was electric; when she made eye contact with him and her eyes flashed, just a little, he felt like she was giving him her complete attention.

"You've heard the rumors," she said.

"I don't need rumors," Ethan said. "I can put two and two together. So can the rest of us."

Grayson just sat smiling, looking at him.

"So," Ethan said, his heart pounding, "who am I going to report to now?"

"It might be you, actually," Grayson said. "If you can answer a few questions."

The dinner turned out to be Ethan's job interview. As they talked, he realized things were far more difficult than they had seemed. If he took the job, he would have to try to bring back the customers who had fled—or replace them. He would have a year, at most, to raise the share price with no further rounds of investor funding.

Most importantly, he would have to develop a new way of working, one that was built on the commitment people felt for the company. He would have to evaluate the existing management team and make sure they were up to the challenge. If they were not, in some cases, like the CFO, they'd have to fill the position.

Ethan hadn't expected this. He had thought that, like most companies in a similar position, the board would bring in a turnaround artist with experience at other major tech firms. He asked about it, and Tanya Grayson simply said, "We checked around. We just know too many horror stories. We think there's more potential upside with you."

The cynical part of his mind snapped, "And I'm a lot cheaper." The self-effacing part of his mind was stunned by the enormity of the compliment, and the creative part immediately began thinking about the changes they could make at Brightpath to get the business back on track. There was also a promotional part of his mind that started composing his autobiography. "I needed a few days to think about it," he might say in the book. "Could I handle this responsibility? Would my performance justify the board's faith in me?" He imagined going home to talk it over with his wife and teenage children.

Honestly, however, he already knew the answer. He knew the top leaders at Brightpath. As CHRO, he'd participated in all their appraisals. He understood their strengths and weaknesses, and he also thought he knew where the gaps might be. He knew the business, probably better than anyone, and he'd been a tech executive before he moved to HR. In a way, he'd been preparing for this chance all his life.

The questions began, and he satisfied Tanya Grayson with his answers. By 8 p.m., when he stepped out for a few minutes to call his wife, he had accepted the position. Because the company was in trouble, the raise in pay wasn't what he had hoped for, and Grayson had acknowledged that. They had to create severance packages for Victor and Jennifer, after all. He had more stock options than he'd had before and a few other perks, but the greatest perk of all was the job itself. He would work with people he liked and respected and had the opportunity to bring the business back from this crisis while testing his own leadership skills. He would no longer be just the "people person." He was running the operation. He would need to learn an immense amount in order to succeed. Putting Brightpath back on top would be huge for his reputation, and his future would be set.

Of course, he realized, if he failed, he'd still have a huge reputation—a less enviable one.

He and Tanya Grayson spent the next two hours considering who might fill key roles. They would ask Rajiv Patel, currently the head of finance for Asia, to step into the CFO role that Jennifer had left. He would be the company's first CFO in India, overseeing financial operations from the same Mumbai location. Emma, the chief technology officer (CTO), would remain. She was based in London and would drive product innovation from there, while leaders in marketing and operations remained in the US. Ethan chose his own former deputy, Samira, to be the new CHRO; she was based in the US.

On Thursday, things went as they had hoped. Rajiv and Samira accepted the new roles after Ethan's Zoom call with each of them. Greg, the chief marketing officer (CMO), sat down with Ethan and Tanya in person in a conference room. Greg looked annoyed at first, but he soon reverted to his usual cheerful demeanor. He became more animated when Ethan talked about using the announcement of his new role to demonstrate that Brightpath could respond to problems before they became disasters.

Leah, the vice president (VP) of operations, met with them in the afternoon. She tended to be circumspect, the kind of person who didn't like to promise anything before she was sure she could deliver. This time, she smiled warmly and said she was glad. She had been sending out her résumé and now she was relieved with the news, and she agreed to stay.

They announced Ethan's new appointment to the staff and the press on Friday. They followed that with a conference call for the board and key shareholders. Ethan went home early on Friday so he would have time to prepare. His first big meeting as CEO, with the executive team, would begin first thing Monday morning.

MONDAY

The soft hum of the elevator doors broke the silence as they opened onto the fifteenth floor of the Brightpath headquarters building. Ethan Caldwell stepped out, taking in the familiar sight of the bright, modern office space. It was the same space he had come to every day, but it felt fresh and new entering it today as the CEO.

At Brightpath, Ethan was seen as a visionary. He could talk passionately about the evolution of the workforce and the company's ability to inspire others. The hybrid nature of Brightpath, with half of its workforce in corporate offices spread across various time zones and continents and the other half working remotely, presented unique challenges—challenges he knew he could overcome. Still, the weight of the role settled on him as he walked toward Victor's old office, which was now his.

Ethan and Rajiv, the new CFO, had spent much of the weekend going through the financial reports. The crisis was bad, but the worst part of it was the way Victor and Jennifer had tried to hide the damage from the board. A number of projects had missed deadlines or gone over budget, and the company was behind on collecting payments from clients. If they couldn't deliver existing orders, collect outstanding payments from customers, and bring in at least one new account within three months, they would have to lay people off.

The only saving grace was that by isolating their activity and keeping it hidden, Victor and Jennifer had not damaged the rest of the company too much. Nobody else seemed to be complicit. And now that it was all out in the open, they could bring the entire firm together to develop a path forward—if they could figure out how to act cohesively.

Ethan had scheduled a full day of meetings, including all morning with the executive team. He was rehearsing his opening remarks in his office, looking down at his notes, when Andrea, Victor's executive assistant who would report to him as the new CEO, interrupted his thoughts.

"Here's your schedule, Ethan," she said with a smile, handing him a piece of paper. "After the executive team meeting, you have a meeting with the product development leads, and then Ms. Grayson at four o'clock in the afternoon. Would you like coffee?"

"Thanks, Andrea. Coffee sounds great."

At Brightpath, only the CEO had an executive assistant. Ethan had used the admin pool to schedule meetings and submit expenses, and he had done the rest himself. He wasn't even sure he should keep Andrea. But how could he let her go? She probably knew more about Victor's history than anyone else there.

But he could change the atmosphere a bit. "Just call Ms. Grayson Tanya," he said to Andrea. "Even the board chair gets to be called by her first name here."

"I'm not sure I feel comfortable doing that," she said, smiling at him.

"How about using her first and last name, then?"

"Tanya Grayson?"

Ethan nodded. "It's a small thing. But it's important. People need to feel that we're all in this together, even the board."

He walked into his new office and closed the door. He needed a moment to take it all in. The office was immaculate, with floor-to-ceiling windows overlooking the bustling city below. On one wall was a large screen showing live updates on the company's global operations—teams across North America, Europe, and Asia collaborating virtually. The hybrid nature of the company was clear even in the office setup, with a mix of traditional desks and video conferencing booths for remote meetings.

Ethan sat down and opened his laptop. He had barely signed in when a notification popped up from Emma, the company's chief technology officer, based in London: *"Looking forward to the meeting today. Let's talk strategy after!"*

He smiled. Emma was direct and results-driven, someone he knew he could count on. But he didn't know the other members of the executive team as well, and that's where his focus would be today—understanding how they could work together to make tough decisions.

At ten o'clock sharp, Ethan entered the executive conference room. Emma was already present by video. Also visible on the screen was Rajiv, the CFO, who dialed in from Mumbai. The rest of the team was present in person: Greg, the chief marketing officer (CMO), who was also in charge of sales; Leah, the VP of operations; Samira, the new VP of HR; and Obie, based in Lagos, who ran their emerging markets consultancy group. There were also seven or eight chief subject matter team leaders, experts on the work they did for clients, with projects ranging from SAP to robotics to semiconductor fabrication.

"Good morning, everyone," Ethan said as he took his new seat at the head of the table. "Thank you for being here. I know it's been a transitional time for the company, and I'm looking forward to working together as I move forward in this new role."

The room was quiet as the team studied him, measuring the leader in front of them. He could sense their cautious optimism; he had never done anything that would make them resent him. On the other hand, they had never seen him operate as a leader outside his previous HR function. There was also the uncertainty that came with any major leadership change, compounded by the doubts about their financial future.

"I've been thinking a lot about the unique challenges of this moment," Ethan began. "I'm not going to sugarcoat how bad things are. The viability of our company has been thrown into question. So far, the board supports us, but if someone made a good offer to acquire Brightpath, I'm not sure their confidence would hold. If we want to hold on to this company and regain our status and position, we've got a lot of work to do. This is a brutal situation."

He was heartened to see everyone nodding. On the screen, Emma's thin lips curved upward, just a bit.

"If we want to grow further, competence at our current level is essential—but it's not going to be enough. Our reputation took a hit. We're in a field that's changing faster than ever, and we need to raise our game to rebuild our business and keep up. The board hired me because they trust in my ability to lead us forward, and I'm committed to earning that trust every step of the way."

Now came the tough part. Ethan took a sip of water and continued, "We all had concerns about Victor's leadership style. But we kept quiet. We didn't even talk to each other about it. I think it's because we didn't know who to trust. It turned out that he and Jennifer weren't honest with us. That's because we—and the board—gave him a blank check. He didn't tell us what he was doing. We didn't hold him accountable for the way he treated people, and that made him feel it was OK to abuse the company."

"You link his personal behavior to the company's problems," said Leah. It was more of a question than a comment.

"Of course I do," said Ethan. "When the top leader is untrustworthy, it pollutes the whole system. None of us could make clear decisions. If I had known I would have to clean up Victor's mess, I would have designed the appraisal system differently. And I probably would have recruited different types of people."

The next thing he said wasn't from his script.

"Leah, consider the question you just asked and the answer I gave you. We would never have talked that openly when Victor led the meetings. We were all trying to look good. It was subtle, but it affected everything we said and everything we did." He paused. "I hope we can continue to communicate more honestly and directly now."

They all nodded, but he noticed that only the CMO was looking directly at him. That made sense: Greg had a confrontational side, and his smile sometimes took on a sharp edge, as if he was holding back an urge to bite. Everyone else looked uncomfortable, but no one said anything, and Ethan moved on.

"We are all going to have to become more effective leaders," Ethan continued. Now he went back to his notes. This was his opportunity to set the tone for his tenure as CEO. "And look, I believe in leading by example. I believe in a leadership style where we're serving each other and the company's mission. It is no longer enough for any of us just to manage tasks. That means creating an environment where we hold each other accountable and also trust one another to get the job done. No one should ever feel left out or unheard. And no one is above criticism or verification, even the CEO."

Heads nodded again around the table, but he could sense that some remained skeptical. It was as if the old system, the system under Victor, had beaten them down. Ethan soldiered on.

"We need to deal with a couple of issues right away. First, we're doing a full audit of what happened. Rajiv, you'll have to lead that personally."

Rajiv nodded. "I was expecting this. I've begun to set up the task force."

"Thank you. We can't afford any more surprises," Ethan continued. "I want everyone in the company to cooperate with you. If they don't, tell me. In fact, we should probably check in every few days."

"I'll put it on our calendars," Rajiv said.

Ethan nodded and moved on. "Second, we must try to win back the customers we lost. We can't do that unless we can demonstrate we've got something special to offer. We're going to have to beef up our innovation and services portfolio, and I think we need to loosen up the structure of our client teams. That means we need better incentives. We have to change how we hire and promote our people."

Greg raised his hand. "Can I say something?"

"Sure," Ethan said after a moment of disorientation. He had just been getting started.

"Those clients are gone," Greg said. "I can't promise to get them back. And it would take a lot of expense to try. We have better prospects for replacing them instead."

"We have to try," Ethan said. "Even if they don't come—even if we fail, we'll learn from it."

Greg waved his hand dismissively, almost in spite of himself, but then dropped his hand, sat back in his chair, and looked attentively at Ethan again.

"Third, I've been looking at the places where we can start changing the way we do things. For instance, we're at a critical juncture with remote work. We're hybrid—part office-based, part remote, and also global. It's a model that has enormous potential, but it also comes with challenges."

Ethan looked around the room and then deliberately focused his attention on Emma, Rajiv, and Obie, who were looking at him impassively from the screen. Ethan had no idea what they were thinking.

"Look at our team right now. We've had this issue for years, ever since Victor implemented Webex. Emma, we're at the end of your day. Same with you, Obie. Rajiv, you'll be here until two o'clock in the morning your time."

"I took a nap. I'm used to it," Rajiv said, smiling. He always seemed at ease.

"I'm just commenting on your flexibility. And when we schedule meetings when it's nighttime here, we're flexible too. Our commitment to the company is obvious. And yet, when we talk through Zoom, people seem checked out—even at this level. I've been part of lively discussions where people get really excited and creative together. These meetings are fine, but they're not lively. We have to find a way to change that. If the top executive team can't communicate effectively, imagine how the project teams throughout the company are doing."

Emma, the CTO in London, nodded in agreement. "I've seen that, too. People are checking out, especially in remote meetings. We need to find a way to make everyone feel more accountable and invested."

"That's exactly right," Ethan said. "It starts with us. First, we'll set the tone and then lead by example. Without our engagement, we cannot expect our teams to be engaged. We can't allow poor communication to become the norm."

He was pleased to see them all sitting up. "My priority as your CEO," he continued, "is to bridge these gaps, to make sure everyone—whether you're in this room, on a video call, or working from across the world—feels connected and empowered."

Leah raised her hand, but Ethan signaled that he still had more to say.

"Today, I want to hear from each of you. What's working well, and what's not? What challenges do you face with your teams, especially in this hybrid environment? The more I know, the better I can serve you as your leader."

As he opened the floor for discussion, Ethan noticed Leah was the first to speak up.

"We've been doing well on the operations side," she said. "But there's a disconnect with some of the global project teams. Communication isn't always smooth, and I think it's affecting what we deliver."

"I've seen that, too," Greg, the CMO, chimed in. "The marketing team feels disconnected from our international teams. We've got great ideas coming from multiple teams and locations, but there's no process for integrating all the input. I'm worried we're missing opportunities."

Ethan asked them for more details, and they started going through cases. There were teams who had lost bids after months of work. There were missed deadlines or projects that had gone way over budget, with nobody held accountable. There were also triumphs, but the teams never got recognized or promoted—and then seemed to lose interest. These were the kinds of issues Ethan was expecting to hear, and he gathered many examples of cases they could analyze in greater detail to guide the development of better processes. By the end of the meeting, Ethan had heard from every executive. Some were more vocal than others, but he now had a clearer picture of the hurdles ahead.

He kept taking notes, and by the time the meeting was done, he had a list of fifty-three top-priority issues. Some were technical, like the problems of getting access to cloud servers around the world. Many were operational team issues, like confusion around the flow of work. The majority had to do with team or individual behavior: there were concerns about leaders who didn't keep up with company expectations. Ethan was determined to tackle these challenges head-on, one by one, so the executive team could set an example. He would go through the list, figure out who was best equipped to handle each challenge, and appoint that person as the problem-fixer. Then he'd dedicate himself to making sure each of those people had the support they'd need.

Before closing the meeting, Ethan addressed the room with one final comment: "As we move forward, I want to emphasize this: the board hired me because they trust me to lead this company through these challenges, and now I need that same trust from all of you. If we commit to this process together—if we take it seriously—I'm confident we'll get through this. Let's make this the moment we turn things around."

Everyone agreed. There were hints of enthusiasm, but by and large, Ethan felt as if people were still processing the shock of Victor's sudden departure and Ethan's promotion to CEO.

Returning to his office, he felt the weight of what lay ahead. Most of these issues couldn't be fixed quickly. They would require a revitalization of the company culture. Everyone would have to understand their role in the bigger picture, no matter where they worked. Leading by example would require more than words. It would demand deliberate actions and unwavering commitment.

SETTING PRIORITIES

Ethan spent the next hour going through the notes he had taken during the leadership meeting. Communication gaps, inefficiencies, and a lack of cohesion across teams were all quietly eroding productivity. And, perhaps more worryingly, this was undermining Ethan's efforts to build a "comeback culture."

He was particularly concerned about the hybrid work model. It should have been their strength, allowing Brightpath to leverage talent from across the world. And yet, it was becoming a weakness, with employees unsure of where they stood in the hierarchy. Were the in-office employees getting more attention? Did remote workers feel overlooked, or worse, expendable? It was time to tackle this head-on.

Ethan knew he couldn't just issue a company-wide memo and expect things to change. The culture had to shift, and that started with him. He had to lead by example.

He expected to learn a lot from his next appointment. He was sitting in on a video call with the product development team—a group primarily made up of remote workers spread across multiple countries, working on a global digital service offering tailored to countries in central Asia and sub-Saharan Africa. Obie would be leading the call, even though it was now close to ten o'clock at night his time. He would introduce Ethan but let everyone know that the CEO was just there as an observer: not to micromanage but to see how things were functioning on the ground or, in this case, over the internet.

The video screen flickered to life, and one by one, faces appeared—half a dozen team members calling in from Berlin, Nairobi, Toronto, Singapore, Bangalore, and Tokyo. Ethan noticed right away how the meeting was unfolding. It was a standard weekly check-in, but the energy felt flat. Everyone seemed to go through the motions, reporting their progress in a disjointed way. There was no spark of collaboration, no real engagement. Most of them were multitasking—checking emails, looking distracted.

It hit Ethan—this was exactly what Greg and Emma had described in the executive meeting. This sense of disconnect wasn't just a side effect of remote work; it was becoming a part of the culture. And if this was happening at the team level, it wouldn't be long before it would bleed into the company's core.

He muted his microphone and observed silently for the rest of the meeting. The team lead wrapped things up after thirty minutes, and everyone signed off as quickly as they had joined. Ethan felt unsettled. This type of meeting and ineffective interactions were exactly what he needed to address.

The rest of the day was packed with more administrative and procedural details. There were a shocking number of procedures to deal with, especially for someone promoted from within, even at an entrepreneurial company like this one. Many of those procedures had been put in place by people in the legal or financial functions. Others came from members of his own staff at HR. He felt like he would need a chief of staff to streamline procedures and weed out unnecessary noise. It was odd, he thought, that Victor had never had one.

At six o'clock in the evening, he met Tanya Grayson. At her request, they met at the Embarcadero, where she had booked a private room. Ethan grabbed a streetcar to get there; it was faster, at this hour, than a cab would be. The streets were getting back to the same level of crowdedness as before the pandemic.

They were on a high floor on the West Side, so the evening light from the sunset flooded in across the rooftops. Ethan sat across from Tanya Grayson, his tie loosened after his first full day as CEO.

"How was day one?" Tanya asked.

Ethan pulled out a notebook filled with hastily scrawled notes from his day of meetings. "Challenging," he admitted. "After two meetings, I had a list of fifty-three issues that need attention. But then I narrowed them down to twelve top priorities." He began listing them off: "Engineering and product teams are misaligned. I think that's partly because of the remote work and partly because we haven't had training in team facilitation. Sales teams can't make reliable promises to clients, and I want to talk with Greg about setting up a better link with production. Nobody seems ready to make a decision. They all seem to default to asking their leader for help. We need to model taking initiative, but I think the executive team has the same problem. We've got irregular reporting practices to clean up from Victor's tenure, and I've asked Rajiv to set up a task force. It's too sensitive for outside consultants, but I'm not sure finance has the bandwidth…"

Tanya sat listening, taking a few notes herself as he talked through the top twelve priorities. For each one, he had an idea about the root cause and a solution.

When he was finished, he looked at her, as if for approval.

"It's too much," she said. "Your own initiative is great. But you're making it much too complicated."

Ethan paused. "Well, as CEO—"

"Actually." Tanya leaned forward, her voice carrying a hint of steel that came from decades in venture capital. "As CEO, you'll never be able to solve all these problems at once. All these issues you've listed? They would require your full attention, and you probably only have enough time for three pillars."

Ethan's interest was piqued. After a day of feeling overwhelmed by the sheer number of challenges, the prospect of a simpler framework was appealing. "What do you mean by pillars?"

"I mean three big changes that hold up the rest."

"And you already know what those should be?"

"Yes, of course. I've seen so many companies come and go, and these are the big three for just about all of them." Tanya held up one finger. "First, trust. Your people need to trust each other, and they need to trust leadership. After what happened with Victor and Jennifer moving R&D funds around and hiding problems from the board, trust has been shattered. Consider that fear you mentioned about people being afraid to make decisions. It's a symptom of broken trust."

Ethan nodded.

"Second," she continued, raising another finger, "accountability. We need clear roles and responsibilities, and people need to own their parts of the business. Right now, everyone's pointing fingers because nobody's sure who's responsible for what. That's why you're getting conflicting stories from engineering and production and why sales can't make commitments."

"And the third pillar?" Ethan prompted, already seeing how these concepts could be mapped out to solve the challenges he'd observed.

"Communication," Tanya stated firmly. "Especially with your global, hybrid workforce, you need robust channels for sharing information, aligning on goals, and staying connected. The disconnect between your international offices and headquarters? The misunderstandings between teams? Those are communication problems at their core."

Ethan felt a weight lifting from his shoulders. The challenges hadn't disappeared, but suddenly, they seemed more manageable. "So instead of fifty separate problems..."

"You have three areas of focus," Tanya finished. "Trust, accountability, and communication. Every issue on that list can be traced back to one or more of these pillars. Fix these three foundational issues, and the rest will follow."

"But how do I—"

"One step at a time," Tanya interrupted gently. "Start with one or two things and move forward."

"OK, we'll start with trust," Ethan said. "We need that first before we can improve communication and accountability."

By this time, they were on the main course. Ethan had a lamb chop, and Tanya had an eggplant korma dish.

"I think, if anything, trust comes last," she said. "You can't trust people unless you have positive interactions and effective communication with them. And if nobody can be held accountable, then trust never gets real. On the other hand, you have to model being trustworthy right from the beginning."

"You mean—"

"Be transparent about what you know and what you don't know," she said, looking him directly in the eye. "Admit mistakes quickly. Show your people it's safe to do the same." She paused, studying him. "You did this in HR, Ethan. It's why we chose you. You understand that sustainable growth comes from investing in people and building trust."

"So, can you help me? Where do we start?"

"Thanks for the compliment, Ethan, but I can't get directly involved, even if I had the time. The board needs me to keep some distance." Seeing Ethan suppress a frown, she laughed. "Even so, I want to meet regularly if you're OK with it."

"Of course I am," Ethan said. Then right away, he added to show he understood, "So where do *I* start?"

"What you permit, you promote," she replied.

He had seen the statement before, but never paid much attention to it.

"As a leader," Tanya continued, "if you give people a pass for lying to each other, or if you allow things to happen without holding anyone accountable, or if you let half-hearted communications slide, you are, in effect, endorsing these things. And people will think these behaviors are acceptable, and they'll do them too."

"We have rules about all those things," Ethan said. "With a mandatory annual quiz for employees." He didn't mention it, but as CHRO, he'd been responsible for running the quiz.

"Yes," she said. "I know all about it. And Victor never looked at the results unless there was someone he wanted to get rid of."

"So, you're saying push the quiz harder," he said, looking at her.

"No," she said, her smile so wide and toothy that it was practically a grin. "I'm saying be so clear and firm that the quiz isn't needed, and you don't need to enforce the rules. And then figure out one thing to do on trust, one thing on communication, and one thing on accountability. Do those first, see what happens, and then pick another thing for each. Move the needle forward a little bit each time."

"The board brought me in to fix things quickly," Ethan said, voicing the concern that had been nagging at him all day. "Will they have the patience for this kind of fundamental rebuilding?"

Tanya sat back, smoothing her blazer. "The board brought you in because we believe in your ability to transform this company. We've seen the damage that short-term thinking can do." She fixed on him with her intense gaze. "Remember what I told you last week? This isn't just about saving Brightpath. If you can pull this off—if you can show that promoting a CHRO to CEO and focusing on the human side of leadership can turn a company around—you'll be setting a new standard that could influence the other companies we invest in."

As they finished their dinner, Ethan felt a renewed sense of purpose. The list of problems in his notebook hadn't changed, but his perspective had. He went home to tell his wife about his first day as CEO. Tomorrow, he would begin rebuilding Brightpath's foundations, one pillar at a time.

He woke with excitement to get to the office and get started. Ethan stood up from his desk and paced the room. He needed to act swiftly, but with purpose. His first step could be to change the way team meetings were conducted. The team needed to feel connected, valued, and responsible, no matter where they were working from. And that meant setting higher expectations—both for himself and the company.

He knew it wasn't enough to just address the product development team's disconnect; the leadership needed to be aligned first.

WHAT WE PERMIT

Ethan called for an impromptu meeting with his executive team. Everyone was able to make time on their calendar the following day. By that time, Ethan had been able to observe a few more staff meetings, including one aimed at recovering a lost client and another that was beginning an audit. The technical and financial issues were complex, but just as daunting were the dynamics of the teams themselves. People seemed cautious, suspicious of one another, and unwilling to make decisions. Every issue seemed to fit into the same key themes: lack of accountability, lack of trust, and an inability to communicate.

"Thanks for joining on short notice, everyone," Ethan began as the last team member arrived on the video call. "I wanted to follow up on our last discussion. I've been sitting in on a few mid-level global team meetings this week," he continued. "They're all hybrid meetings, with people calling in on Zoom from all over the world. They're all with different groups, but I noticed something concerning. There's a lack of engagement. People seem to go through the motions, but they don't volunteer anything, and they don't seem to grasp the challenges we're facing. It's clear to me that we need to address this immediately, and I say this group is accountable. Whatever we decide to do on this team, I'll make sure it happens."

Somehow, that last remark seemed to unlock people's willingness to speak up. Emma, the CTO, was the first. "I've seen the same thing in the engineering teams. A few people contribute, but most don't speak. As for the remote teams, they barely participate. It's like they're on an island of their own."

Greg, the CMO, added, "It's not just engineering. The marketing department also feels it. I know what you mean about going through the motions."

Leah, the VP of operations, chimed in next. "It's not just the meeting format. It's the whole culture here. I don't think we realize how these scandals have affected all of us." Leah was known for being hard-headed and uninterested in the "fluff" of management; it was unusual for her to mention culture at all. The room's energy seemed to shift.

Ethan nodded. "Exactly, and here's the thing—I talked with Tanya about it, too. Or, rather, she pointed it out to me. She reminded me of that old saying: what we permit, we promote. Victor permitted employees to be secretive and deceptive because he was all those things himself. And even though we didn't know the details of what was happening at the highest levels, the culture of the company was shaped by those dishonest practices."

"We definitely feel the negative effects of the company's culture in finance," Rajiv said. "Employees test the limits and want to know what they can get away with."

"OK then," Ethan said. He struggled to maintain his composure as he got more frustrated with what he was hearing. "Starting this week, we're going to be very deliberate about what we permit. If we allow disengagement and lack of communication to continue, we are essentially promoting a culture of suspicion and incompetence, even if we don't mean to. We need to make sure that everyone feels equally valued and accountable, no matter where they are in the world."

Greg leaned forward, intrigued. "So, what's the plan?"

"Before we can establish and enforce rules," Ethan replied, "we need to set an example. Remember when I mentioned leadership by example? We're going to take that seriously. I'll be closely monitoring how each of you in this room communicates with your team going forward, and you are responsible for setting the new standards for everyone else in the company."

Now he had everyone's attention. "First, we'll tighten up how we conduct meetings, especially in this hybrid environment. We're done with passive check-ins. From now on, every meeting needs to have an explicit purpose and desired outcomes. I want this group to set an example. When we're engaged, our teams will follow."

"That means we will need to know the purpose of the meeting in advance," Emma said.

"Exactly," Ethan replied. "I'll send the agenda out to you all each week. Eventually, we'll rotate the moderatorship, so you're all in the hot seat."

"But that's not enough," Greg added.

Ethan held up his hand in agreement. "Yes. We need to establish clear lines of accountability for both in-office and remote employees. Everyone needs to know what's expected of them, no matter where they're working from."

Samira, the new VP of HR (and Ethan's replacement), chimed in for the first time. "And we need to make sure that accountability isn't perceived as micromanaging. It's about building trust, right? Remote workers need to feel like they're a valued part of the team, not second-class employees."

"Exactly," Ethan said. "Accountability and trust go hand in hand. We need to show our teams that we trust them to deliver, but we also need to make sure everyone—whether they're working remotely or in the office—feels equally responsible for the company's success."

Ethan realized it was essential to clarify what trust truly meant for Brightpath. "Trust isn't just some vague ideal," Ethan said. "It's the cornerstone of everything we're building here. To me, trust means a mutual belief in each other's reliability, integrity, and intentions. It's about knowing that we can count on one another to communicate openly, deliver on commitments, and act in the best interests of the team."

Ethan paused for a moment before he continued. "As leaders, building trust means setting high standards and being consistent in our actions and communications so that everyone feels secure and valued, whether they're here in the office or working remotely. If we don't clearly define what we mean by trust and demonstrate those qualities in our interactions with other employees, our partners, and our customers, we'll never have the cohesion we need to be successful."

"So, if we see something happening that isn't in line with our new standards—with accountability, trust, or communication—we have to call it out?" asked Samira.

"Not only do you call it out directly to the employee," Ethan said, "but you raise it here too. We won't penalize anyone while we're establishing these new standards, but we all have to know what's going on."

"We'll have to track these interactions," Samira said. "If you all agree, I think this could fall under HR. Sooner or later, it will feed into performance appraisals. I can manage the data."

Ethan felt a twinge of annoyance. He would never have volunteered like that when Victor ran the company. Victor liked to make every decision. But Ethan's impulse to snap back immediately faded. This was exactly the kind of initiative he wanted people to take. He wanted his executive team to feel empowered to make suggestions and help implement the changes.

"OK then," he said. "I think we've got our first new case study."

As the meeting progressed, Ethan felt a renewed sense of hope. He could see that the executive team was on board with the changes he was proposing. The culture shift wouldn't happen overnight, but they were moving in the right direction.

As the meeting wrapped up, Ethan made one last point. "Remember, this isn't just about meetings or communication protocols. This is about how we lead. This week, remember the significance of what we permit, we promote. Think about what that looked like when Victor was in charge and what we want it to look like now going forward. If we want this company to thrive in a hybrid world, we need to set the bar high—starting with ourselves."

That evening, Ethan felt a sense of clarity he hadn't experienced since accepting the CEO role. Leading by example wasn't just about showing up or being visible. It was about setting standards, holding people accountable, and making sure that every decision, no matter how small, aligned with the values he wanted to instill throughout the company. If he permitted disconnection, disengagement, or lack of accountability, those behaviors spread. But if he promoted trust, responsibility, and clear communication, those values would take root.

The next day, he would begin setting those values into motion—starting with himself.

SHIFTING THE CULTURE

The following Monday, the executive team met again. A lot had happened. Victor and Jennifer had resurfaced long enough to receive a preliminary indictment and notice of investigation for fraud. The board had issued a statement, which Tanya, Ethan, and Greg (representing marketing) had spent a day crafting. It read:

FOR IMMEDIATE RELEASE

Brightpath Solutions Announces Leadership Changes Following Internal Investigation

SAN FRANCISCO—Brightpath Solutions ("Brightpath" or "the Company") has announced that following an internal investigation supported by external counsel and forensic accountants, the Company has terminated Victor Andrews as chief executive officer and Jennifer Morris as chief financial officer, effective immediately.

The investigation, initiated by the Board of Directors, uncovered irregularities in the Company's financial reporting and R&D fund allocations. The Company has reported these findings to relevant authorities and is cooperating fully with their ongoing investigation.

"Brightpath is committed to maintaining the highest standards of corporate governance and financial integrity," said Tanya Grayson, chairperson of the board. "We are taking decisive action to address these issues and strengthen our internal controls."

The board has appointed Ethan Caldwell, previously chief human resources officer, as CEO and Rajiv Patel, formerly VP of finance in Asia, as CFO. The new leadership team is implementing additional oversight measures and will focus on reinforcing the Company's commitment to transparency and ethical business practices.

The Company does not expect these changes to impact its ability to serve its clients or deliver on its commitments. Brightpath maintains a strong market position and will continue to provide industry-leading software solutions to its global customer base.

The announcement listed Greg as head of corporate communications and directed further communications to him. Ethan had proposed adding a reference to the company's cultural values: trust, accountability, and communication. But Tanya had said they weren't ready yet to claim these values externally.

Ethan spent almost as much time working out the agenda for the weekly executive team meeting. As he'd said, all eyes would be on them, and that meant he had to strike just the right note: neither too domineering nor too passive. He had shared this with the team three days before the meeting and again during the beginning of the meeting:

> **Purpose:** To clarify our priorities for Brightpath's transformation during the next one hundred days.
>
> **Agenda:**
>
> Communication
>
> > Practice Transparent Communication
> >
> > Elevate Remote Team Visibility
>
> Accountability
>
> > Establish Clear Accountability
>
> Trust
>
> > Hold Trust-Building Conversations
>
> **Outcome:** A clear, simple statement of purpose with up to four action steps for the whole company to follow.

Samira, the VP of HR, looked thoughtful. She was across the table from Ethan, and he could see she was choosing her words carefully. "I think part of the problem is that we don't have consistent guidelines for hybrid work. Some managers are doing regular check-ins with their remote teams, but others aren't. We need to standardize how we handle communication and accountability."

"You're right," Ethan replied. "We need to set clear expectations, and it starts with us. I'm going to hold myself accountable, and I expect each of you to do the same. We need to show our teams that we're committed to making this new approach work—and that means leading by example."

He paused, glancing around the room to gauge their reactions. The team seemed engaged, but he could tell they were waiting for something concrete, something actionable. Ethan leaned forward, his tone shifting from reflective to determined.

"As I shared with you on the agenda, I've outlined four immediate actions I want us to implement. I need to know what you think about them. I want your help to improve them, and then I need your full support."

ACTION 1: PRACTICE TRANSPARENT COMMUNICATION

"Transparency is critical," Ethan said, shifting everyone's focus. "Every conversation should start with clear intentions and include the 'why.' Why is this task important? Why does it matter to the team, the company, or the mission? When employees understand the reasoning behind decisions, they feel more connected and motivated."

Rajiv, the CFO, added, "Transparency isn't just about information—it's about context. If people don't understand the bigger picture, they can't fully commit to their roles."

"That's exactly right," Ethan affirmed. "We also need to foster two-way communication. Feedback should flow both ways, whether it's during a team meeting or a one-on-one. When teams feel heard, it strengthens trust and creates an environment where transparency thrives."

"Why put this one first?" asked Leah. "It seems pretty abstract. How are we going to enforce it?"

"Thank you, Leah. That's a great example of exactly what I mean," Ethan said. "From now on, I intend to include the 'why' in what I say—and if I don't, please remind me. There's always a 'why' there."

"It's because of Victor, isn't it?" asked Samira.

Ethan wondered how many other people in the company felt the same way and had been wondering the same thing. While working within a company culture that didn't feel safe, she probably had felt subtly squelched, time after time. "Victor, and Jennifer, and anyone who doesn't explain the reasons for what they're doing," he replied. "We can't enforce it—but we can model it. And it's like a working hypothesis. I believe it will have a positive influence on our ability to dig ourselves out of this mess."

Greg raised his hand, a habit left over from school. "You wrote we should 'practice' transparency. Shouldn't we just do it? Why do we need to practice?"

"Because we're implementing this as a new habit," Ethan said. "It will take some practice before it becomes second nature."

ACTION 2: ELEVATE REMOTE TEAM VISIBILITY

"This action also falls under communication," Ethan told the group. "We need to make sure our remote employees are just as visible and involved as those in the office. This means rethinking how we run meetings. From now on, every meeting—whether it's a quick check-in or a strategic discussion—needs to include all relevant parties, no matter where they're located. Remote employees can't be an afterthought."

Emma nodded in agreement. "We've been guilty of that, especially when meetings are planned on short notice. Sometimes, we assume remote team members can catch up later, but that's part of the problem. They need to be part of the conversation from the start."

"Exactly," Ethan said. "Being visible also means the remote team members have their video on during every meeting. We'll also start rotating meeting leadership between remote and in-office employees. If a remote employee is leading a meeting, they'll naturally feel more integrated, and the rest of the team will see them as a vital part of the process."

ACTION 3: ESTABLISH DEFINED ACCOUNTABILITY

Next, Ethan turned to the topic of accountability. "Defined accountability is the backbone of a high-performing organization. That starts with setting measurable goals and expectations for everyone, and they must be uniform across all teams."

Rajiv nodded. "In the past, teams felt disconnected from major decisions. That meant responsible teams were not held accountable for their actions."

Ethan acknowledged the point. "That's a good point. Moving forward, we'll address that by implementing department-wide accountability frameworks. Goals will be transparent, so everyone will know the process and who is in charge of each step. And we'll ensure regular, structured check-ins focused on outcomes, not activity. Accountability isn't about micromanaging; it's about creating clarity and empowering people to own their responsibilities and meet deadlines."

Samira, the VP of HR, raised a question. "How will we ensure remote team members get the same level of visibility and recognition that in-office staff do?"

Ethan responded confidently. "We'll use technology and structured reporting to track individual and team contributions, but we must move beyond metrics alone. Accountability should feel like a shared commitment, not a top-down mandate."

"So, we're going to do a lot of top-down communication," Greg said.

"Yes," Ethan said. "We have to retrain our direct reports to run their departments and teams so that everyone feels accountable." He turned back to Samira. "You and I will sit down and put together some processes for tracking this. And we need to roll them out within days, not weeks—so clear your calendar."

ACTION 4: FOSTER TRUST

"Trust is the foundation of any successful team," Ethan continued. "But in a high-pressure environment, it can erode quickly if we're not intentional about maintaining it. Building trust starts with communication. Beginning today, every leader in this room must prioritize one-on-one check-ins with their direct reports—especially remote employees. These aren't performance reviews; they're conversations. Ask each member of your team what they need, what challenges they're facing, and how we can better support them."

Leah, the VP of operations, leaned forward. "That's an area where we've fallen short. We might think everything's okay if we check in with people often, but we need to make more of an effort to maintain our relationships."

Ethan smiled. "Thanks, Leah. Yes, that's a good reminder. Engagement, not assumptions, builds trust. As leaders, we need to embrace what's called servant leadership, ensuring our teams have everything they need to succeed, no matter where they're located. We cannot mandate trust, but we can take steps to earn it through intentional, ongoing efforts."

They went on to discuss what servant leadership might look like at Brightpath. Talking about the concept felt awkward because it had never been part of the ethos before. Technicians had reported to team leaders. Team leaders, in turn, had reported to the senior functional and department leaders—the people at this meeting. It was a relatively flat organization, but it wasn't based on servant leadership by any means. Everyone had relied on cues from their bosses, and the bosses were too busy to provide many.

"The teams are not going to get this," Obie said, looking down at them through the webcam. "Unless I know exactly what to tell them."

"Yes," said Emma. Her window was next to his on the screen.

The executive team wrapped up the meeting by refining the language for these four points and confirming that they all agreed these four elements were good first priorities. They set a deadline for one month to come back and assess their progress on each one.

As they walked back out to the corridor, Ethan felt a sense of optimism. The steps were small but meaningful, and he could already see the shift in the room. His team was ready to act. The new management approach would not be a stumbling block for Brightpath. He felt confident that the managers were well-prepared to introduce the new strategies to their teams, and at the one-month check-in, he expected to hear positive feedback and examples of how teams had embraced the changes.

But the actual test was still ahead. Change wouldn't happen overnight. It would take time and a great deal of attention to undo the financial damage and even more to rebuild their reputation. Yet Ethan knew they had already made a genuine start. He'd have to keep pushing, keep leading by example, and keep promoting the values he wanted to see reflected in each of the managers and the employees.

What they permit, they promote. And Ethan wasn't about to let complacency take root.

THE FINANCE STORY

Trust and Accountability

It was the day after the second executive team meeting, and Rajiv Patel hadn't gotten much sleep. He sat at his desk in the quiet of his Mumbai home office, the early-morning sunlight barely peeking through the curtains. The decor was a mix of personal and professional—stacks of financial reports sat next to a photo of his family on the desk, their smiling faces a bittersweet reminder of why he was here.

A few years ago, Rajiv's life had been different. Based in Brightpath's US headquarters, he had been thriving as the VP of Accounting, building strong relationships with his colleagues and enjoying the camaraderie of an in-office environment. But a family health emergency had changed everything. His parents needed him back in India, and Rajiv had made the tough decision to move.

The shift had been manageable. Brightpath had been accommodating to his needs. His new responsibility was overseeing Asian finance, which suited him. The pandemic had forced many staff members into remote work, and his position in India gave him a direct window into the challenges of a global enterprise. His basic routine of handling reports and numbers didn't change all that much, and this provided a comforting stability.

But now he was promoted to CFO overnight, accountable for cleaning up a financial crisis created by his upper management. He suddenly was in charge of leading a global team split between outsourced accounting operations in India, a finance team in the US, and finance leaders in the other six main offices. Right out of the gate, he had to lead them through a rapid forensic investigation—assembling and auditing financials that his predecessor had hidden from view.

The hours were brutal, and having to manage multiple time zones made it worse. Rajiv often found himself on early-morning calls with the US team and late-night discussions with the outsourced accountants. Everyone had to retrace transactions they had quickly signed off on based on Jennifer's assurances. Some were valid, and others had—well, murky provenance.

The cultural gaps added another layer of complexity. The US team spoke directly and plainly—or so they thought, according to their cultural standards—but their remarks often came across as dismissive to the India team. The India team's deference to people in authority often frustrated their American counterparts because, at times, it seemed to hold them back from bringing problems to the surface. On the other hand, they tended to find things that the other team ignored.

Rajiv leaned back in his chair, rubbing his temples. A call with Ethan Caldwell, Brightpath's CEO, was on his calendar for later in the day. While Rajiv appreciated Ethan's emphasis on trust and accountability, he wasn't sure how those principles could bridge the divide between his teams—and unless they bridged the divide, he didn't know how they could finish the forensic accounting.

The Finance Story

• • •

The weekly finance and accounting meeting started promptly at eight o'clock in the morning Mumbai time. Rajiv watched as the familiar faces popped onto the video call—on one side, the US finance team sat in their sleek office conference room, dressed in business casual. On the other, the India accounting team appeared in individual video squares, their backgrounds ranging from home offices to brightly lit workstations.

The meeting began with routine updates, but tension quickly bubbled to the surface.

"We're still waiting on the final numbers from the India team," said Mark, a senior analyst on the US side. His clipped tone showed his frustration. "It's causing delays in the audit."

"Final numbers?" asked Priya, the finance lead for the India team. "We sent the data two days ago, but we needed clarification on some line items. We asked for feedback and didn't hear back."

Mark frowned. "We don't have time to go back and forth. We need those numbers on time, period."

Rajiv unmuted his mic, stepping in before the conversation escalated further. "Let's pause here," he said, his voice calm but firm. "It sounds like there's a breakdown in the handoff process. I knew there were issues, but I didn't realize how difficult things were. Is this just related to the audit, or are these chronic problems?"

"We have problems like this every quarter," Priya said.

"Yes, and it's always the same story," Mark responded quickly. "In fact—"

Rajiv quickly interrupted him. Brightpath couldn't afford any further breakdown in communication. "Look," he said. "What we permit, we promote, and we're not going to permit infighting. We can't afford it. We're all accountable for this, and if we're going to finish the audit, we have to do it together. Priya, let's review what information you need from Mark's team to avoid delays in the future."

Priya nodded, but the tension lingered. As the meeting wrapped up, Rajiv couldn't ignore the sense of disconnect between the two groups. The lack of trust and differences in communication style were dragging them down, and it was clear nobody was willing to take responsibility. The solution would require more than just a few process changes.

* * *

Later that day, Rajiv joined his one-on-one call with Ethan. The CEO's face appeared on the screen, his expression warm and attentive.

"Rajiv, good to see you," Ethan said. "How are things on your end?"

Rajiv hesitated, then was honest. "Challenging," he admitted. "The accounting and finance teams are struggling to work together. The US team feels like they're carrying all the responsibility, and the India team feels undervalued. Add in the time zones and cultural differences, and it's been... a lot."

Ethan leaned forward. "I hear you," he said. "It's difficult leading a global team, especially one as diverse as yours, especially under this kind of pressure. What do you think is at the core of the issue?"

"Trust," Rajiv said without hesitation. "The US team doesn't trust the India team to handle things independently, and the India team feels like they're being micromanaged. And since the whole thing started with a breach of trust, no one feels certain about anything."

Ethan nodded. "Trust is foundational, but it needs clarity to thrive. What if you focused on defining roles and responsibilities more explicitly? And maybe create opportunities for the teams to see each other as partners rather than separate groups?"

Rajiv considered this. "It's worth a try," he said. "But that would normally take time, and I know we don't have much of that right now."

"Yeah, I can't cut you any slack on the deadline," Ethan agreed. "But you can make a start. And after all this is over, they'll still have to work together."

"In that case," Rajiv said, "I'm going to need your support to plan the workshop for a full three days. That's a lot of time away from our day-to-day responsibilities."

...

Rajiv sat down with a fresh cup of chai, the faint buzz of the morning in Mumbai providing the background noise. Today marked the beginning of his department's three-day intensive workshop. During the first two days, they would collectively work through the anomalies related to the audit. Then they'd devote the third day to laying the groundwork for the future.

These sessions would redefine how his global team collaborated. He had spent his whole weekend preparing for this moment, reviewing the report they'd produced, and crafting a plan to bridge the gap between the two teams so they could get to the finish line.

The first day brought both teams—US finance and India accounting—together virtually. Rajiv started by addressing the tension directly. His calm, authoritative tone added gravity to his words.

"We've all been feeling the pressure lately," Rajiv began, his gaze sweeping the Brady Bunch-style grid of faces on the screen. "But I believe that part of our challenge lies in not having clear expectations of one another. Today, that is where we are going to start."

He divided the workshop into small breakout sessions, each focused on a specific part of the audit. Each group included a mixture of employees from India, from the US, and those scattered elsewhere. Each team was accountable for finding and analyzing the issues in their domain.

Each team began by producing a statement defining their particular responsibilities and where they might overlap with what the other teams were responsible for completing. Then they began to work, focusing on areas where the data seemed ambiguous or caused confusion.

The workshop hours were staggered to accommodate the time zone differences. They all had to sacrifice some of their early mornings and evenings. Rajiv insisted on keeping the same teams intact, working across the digital divide for two full days, using all the AI tools available to them to hunt down more data oddities. A team of senior leaders—again divided among the US, India, and the rest of the globe—checked each team's conclusions, ran a further AI-based assessment, and proofread the results.

Rajiv had hoped that working on critically important cleanup projects might bring the teams closer together. It was like sending people into a war zone, he thought. He was pleasantly surprised to see signs that some of the cohesion actually took hold.

By the end of the second day, when each group signed off on their sections of the report, the team members were no longer quietly snarling at one another on their webcams. Most were showing their faces, and they seemed eager to send off the results. They understood that they were taking part in a historic moment for the company—and that adapting to the changes was an essential prerequisite for keeping their jobs. Moreover, they had accomplished what they had set out to do. No matter what happened next, each team had proven they could be accountable for an issue of consequence.

With that experience just behind them, Rajiv started the third day with a look at the processes going forward. He used charts with graphics to propose a working model for the company's future financial activities. It included the handoffs between the US and India, a source of persistent friction. He displayed the prototype for a new, streamlined system, incorporating digital tools and proposing new ways to exchange information and context more easily as they shared data and their opinions.

"We need to treat these handoffs as a baton pass in a relay," Rajiv explained, using a sports analogy he knew would resonate with the US team. "It's not just about finishing your part, but ensuring the next person can pick up where you left off to seamlessly complete the next steps in the process."

Rajiv also introduced a shared project tracker—a centralized tool for clearly documenting deadlines, progress updates, and handoff points. Each team would now have access to the same information, eliminating the silos that had caused delays in the past.

To address accountability, Rajiv assigned a point of contact for each critical task. Now, if questions arose or issues emerged, there would always be someone responsible for resolving them.

The India team took the changes in stride, appreciating the clarity it brought to their work. Its members took ownership of tasks like reconciliations, compliance reporting, and initial data preparation.

The US team, initially skeptical, quickly saw the benefits. The Americans focused on forecasting, financial analysis, and presenting reports to leadership and clients.

By the end of the session, there was a new sense of clarity. As Priya, the accounting team lead, shared her closing thoughts, she said, "It feels good to finally know exactly where we stand. This gives us a better understanding of how our work fits into the full end-to-end process."

Mark from the US team nodded in agreement. "It'll make our jobs easier, too, knowing exactly what to expect from the handoffs."

That night, Rajiv typed a quick chat message to Ethan:

> *"The teams look like they can work as one. It will take some time, but I think it will pay off. I can't thank you enough for encouraging me to create opportunities for the teams to see each other as partners rather than separate groups."*

As he hit send, Rajiv glanced at the photo of his family. His journey to India had been unplanned and difficult, but it had taught him resilience and adaptability. Leading a global team wasn't easy, but he thought it would make him a better leader—and perhaps a better person.

THE R&D STORY

Communication and Trust

In Ethan's second week as CEO, he had Emma, the CTO, fly in from London for a week of prototyping sessions. They brought the Bay Area engineers into the office, with groups in London, Singapore, Mumbai, and even Lagos joining via Zoom. This would be the first major test of their comprehensive innovation strategy for the company under its new leadership.

Emma had been one of the most vocal executives regarding the growing communication problems between the remote and in-office teams, especially among the engineering staff. Ethan respected her candor—Emma wasn't afraid to speak up when she saw problems, and that was exactly the directness he needed in the executive team. But he still worried about whether she could put a whole new approach to remote team visibility into place within a few months.

Impromptu international trips were unusual for Brightpath, but it was worth it to have Emma oversee the Bay Area engineers in person. They urgently needed to devise a credible innovation strategy to build back their reputation and hopefully regain the clients they had lost. The best way to do that was to demonstrate an array of upgraded services, including all the things they offered—tech installations, consultation, training, and staff augmentation—in advanced packages.

Since the engineers were scattered around the world, it was critical to form viable hybrid teams. That was proving difficult. It was ironic, Ethan thought. The fact alone that Emma had to fly in showed how difficult it would be.

As he walked into the glass-walled meeting room, he saw Emma already typing away on her laptop, a cup of coffee beside her.

"Morning, Emma, thank you for making the trip," he said, settling into his chair with his own cup of coffee.

"Ethan, good morning! Ready to tackle this hybrid monster we've created?" she said with a half-smile.

Ethan chuckled. "That's the plan. How are your teams responding to the new meeting format?"

"Honestly? Better than I expected. We rotated leadership responsibilities for the last two meetings, and having remote engineers run the show actually energized the team. It's like they suddenly realized that they were in charge—of the agenda now and maybe other things going forward. It forced everyone to engage more."

"That's exactly what I was hoping for," Ethan said. "What about accountability? Are the remote workers stepping up now that they've got more visibility?"

Emma sighed. "It's improving, but we've got a long way to go. Some of the remote folks are still hesitant to speak up during meetings. If they have concerns about prototypes, they bring them up to me after the meeting. I think they're used to feeling sidelined, and it's going to take time to reassure them that we want their participation and boost their confidence before they feel comfortable sharing with the group. But having clear goals for everyone makes a difference. No one can hide behind vague tasks anymore."

"That's what I like to hear," Ethan replied. "This will not be an overnight change. But as long as we're moving in the right direction, we'll get there."

・・・

The hum of conversation and the occasional squeak of a marker on the whiteboard filled Brightpath's innovation lab. Teams gathered around tables cluttered with sticky notes, laptops, and half-drunk cups of coffee. Emma stood at the front of the room, gesturing to a slide projected on the screen behind her.

At each table, there were two large monitors linked to corresponding tables in London, Singapore, Mumbai, and Lagos. Each table also had its own webcams and microphones. There was enough space between the tables that each group could work independently, and yet they could also visit one another, giving the whole room the feel of a collaborative hackathon.

For all the care that had gone into the setup, the most important and daunting factor was not the meeting technology. It was the quality of interaction among the multi-site teams, including a few remote participants signing in solo from other locations. Every table also had at least one participant from marketing and someone from Obie's emerging markets group as well.

Emma had assigned each group a specific challenge to solve, ranging from product design to internal processes. One particularly important project was called Code Bright. It was a group of updates to their most popular client software package. This bread-and-butter offering hadn't been fully updated for a year, and it was a natural fit for generative AI and better cybersecurity protection. Emma's leadership was apparent as she moved between teams, offering input and encouraging collaboration.

The ambiance was one of quiet hubbub, with teams murmuring at each table. Emma had to raise her voice to quiet everyone. "This is our first rapid prototyping session," she began, her voice carrying a mix of excitement and authority. "The goal is simple: tackle big problems by creating small, functional solutions. We're not aiming for perfection—just progress. Let's experiment, collaborate, and iterate. By the end of today, every team should have something to share with the group that moves the needle, even if it's just a rough sketch or a working demo."

Ethan, standing to the side, watched with a small smile. It was going better than Ethan had expected. During one of the first meetings, Emma had suggested the idea of rapid prototyping as a way to tackle the R&D challenges more collaboratively. Ethan had encouraged the idea, pointing out how it could also help build trust across teams. Now, seeing the session in action, he was impressed to see the idea come to life.

At one table, a group of developers and marketers debated the best way to improve user retention for Brightpath's flagship software-as-a-service package. Emma joined them, glancing at a rough wireframe sketched on a tablet.

"This is a great start," she said. "But have you considered how this feature aligns with the customer feedback we've been getting? Marketing, what do you think?"

The marketing lead chimed in, "It's promising, but we'll need to test messaging alongside the functionality to make it resonate."

"Perfect," Emma said, jotting down a note. "Keep that in mind as you refine this. Remember, it doesn't need to be perfect—it just needs to spark the next conversation."

In another corner of the room, there was a group from the finance function working on a prototype for a more efficient reporting tool. The need for it had become apparent during the audit. Rajiv was deeply engaged with them, logged in from Mumbai. Though initially skeptical about participating, he quickly realized the value of the prototype session.

"Why don't we build a simple dashboard mockup?" he suggested. "It doesn't need all the bells and whistles yet—just something to show how the data flows and what the key metrics are."

"That's a great idea," said Priya, his accounting lead. "We can test it with a few sample reports and see how it holds up."

As the day progressed, Emma took a moment to check in with Ethan. "I wasn't sure how this would go," she admitted. "But seeing the energy in this room—it's incredible."

Ethan nodded. "It's not just about the prototypes. It's about showing people how to work together differently. You've nailed it, Emma."

At the end of the day, each team presented their prototypes. Some were rougher than others, but the excitement in the room was palpable. The ideas sparked during the session carried over into side conversations and would inspire follow-up meetings, igniting a wave of momentum across the company.

Emma wrapped up the day with a smile. "Today was just the beginning," she said to the group. "We've shown what's possible when we put trust, creativity, and collaboration at the center of our work. Let's keep building on that."

THE EXECUTIVE TEAM

Laying the Groundwork for Trust

By the end of the third week, Ethan had scheduled one-on-one check-ins with all his direct reports. The conversations were insightful, but they also highlighted just how much work remained to be done. Brightpath's hierarchical model under Victor had allowed them to scale rapidly, but it had also created silos that needed to be broken down, piece by piece.

This was particularly true in marketing. Ethan realized it when he sat down for his one-on-one check-in with Greg, the CMO. Greg had started as a strong supporter of Ethan's initiatives, particularly with communication and making remote workers feel like an integral part of the team. But Ethan could sense there were still challenges in the marketing department—especially with trust and collaboration between the related functions. At Brightpath, the marketing function had grown rapidly, reflecting Victor's belief in a small executive team. Marketing included customer service, data analytics, and sales, with Greg overseeing all of the departments.

"How's it going?" Ethan asked as they settled into the meeting room.

"Busy, as always," Greg said with a grin. "But we're making progress. The team's been adapting to the new accountability measures pretty well."

"Good to hear," Ethan said. "But I get the sense there are still some underlying issues. What's going on?"

Greg ran a hand through his hair and sighed. "Honestly? It's trust. The in-office team still feels like they're carrying more of the load, even though the remote team is doing just as much work. People seem to believe that you're not working hard unless you're in the office."

Ethan nodded. "That's exactly what I was afraid of. Trust in a hybrid model can't be based on proximity—it has to be built on results and accountability."

"And then there are the groups. Marketing and customer service should be working closely together, sharing data, and drawing conclusions. Sales should be eager to connect with both of them. But it's like pulling teeth to get them to talk."

"So, how do we fix this?"

Greg leaned back in his chair. "I think it's going to come down to transparency. We need to show everyone—remote or in-office—that we're all held to the same standards. Although we have accountability measures, we need to improve the remote staff's visibility. Regular updates, clear progress tracking, and a stronger connection between teams all need to be implemented to demonstrate transparency."

"Exactly," Ethan said. "We need to make building trust intentional. It doesn't happen by accident, especially in a hybrid environment. What if we implemented regular cross-team check-ins? The meetings can serve not only to provide project updates but also to build relationships. Get people talking, get them collaborating more."

"I like that. We've been too focused on tasks," Greg said. "It's time to focus on relationships, too."

Ethan made a note to follow up with Greg on the logistics of these cross-team check-ins. You can't build trust in a day, but with the right foundation, you can start turning things around.

· · ·

One of the most enlightening meetings was with Rajiv, the CFO in Mumbai. The finance team had come through on the audit, and Tanya Grayson and the legal team were using it to build the emerging case against Victor. But Rajiv had concerns about the larger cultural shift Ethan was pushing for.

"Ethan, I understand the need for trust and accountability, but it's not going over well," Rajiv said over the video call. "Cultural differences are holding us back in finance. What works for your team in the US may not resonate with people here in India or with the staff in the UK."

"You're absolutely right, Rajiv," Ethan replied. "I don't want to impose a one-size-fits-all approach. What do you suggest?"

Rajiv smiled. "We need to be flexible, but consistent. Trust is universal, but how we build it can vary. For example, my team thrives on clarity and structure. They like having clearly defined roles and expectations, but they also value the personal connection with leadership. They need to know they're seen and heard, even from across the globe."

"That's a good point," Ethan said. "I'll work with you and the other executives to make sure we're adapting our leadership approach based on cultural context. We need to keep the accountability and trust piece strong, but with flexibility in how we implement it."

· · ·

As Ethan reflected on the week's conversations, he realized that building trust in a hybrid model wasn't just about competence: knowing someone could deliver on a task. It was about belief in their engagement, commitment, and value. Whether they were sitting in the office next door or working remotely from halfway across the world, they had to be treated as reliable collaborators. They had to earn that trust but also be given the opportunities to earn it.

Every action, every policy, and every conversation would have to reflect this double-edged relationship: show commitment and earn the trust of others. Keep that up, and you'll succeed at Brightpath.

What we permit, we promote. Now, more than ever, he thought, *we promote trust.*

EMERGING RESISTANCE

Trust and Communication

Ethan stood by the large window of his office, watching the city skyline as the sun dipped over the Golden Gate Bridge. It was now two months after his appointment as CEO. It had been intense—implementing changes, checking in with his executive team, and keeping the energy up as they worked to regain the confidence of the outside world. Progress was steady. Their first new service offerings had been received well, even though they had rushed them through the innovation stage, and they were back on a growth track.

Inside the company, however, things weren't going as smoothly as he had hoped.

He had known there would be resistance. Change was never easy, especially when it threatened established habits. The old management style had allowed people to work independently, sometimes with little oversight, and now he was establishing firm expectations. Trust and accountability were the cornerstones of his leadership, but they required effort and attention that not everyone was prepared to give—not even when the whole company was obviously at risk.

Samira, the VP of HR, alerted him by email to some rumblings from the staff, particularly from a few senior managers who were used to running their teams with minimal interference. They felt that the new accountability measures were too rigid because they took away the autonomy they had enjoyed. Reading between the lines, it was clear they weren't used to the heightened level of transparency that Ethan was pushing for.

He knew they had to address it. So he forwarded the feedback to the executive team over the weekend, one day in advance of their regular Monday meeting.

• • •

The next day, as the executive team members filed into the conference room and logged into the meeting online, he could sense the undercurrent of tension. They had all read the memo, and he knew they were waiting to see how he'd handle it.

Once everyone was present and engaged, Ethan began. "I think we all expected some kind of discomfort among the ranks." He was careful not to voice the word resistance because he was trying to foster trust. "I know this hasn't been easy for everyone, especially with the new expectations around accountability."

Samira spoke first; her tone measured. "I've had a few managers come to me and express concerns that the increased focus on accountability feels like micromanaging. They're used to having more freedom to run their teams the way they see fit, and now they feel like they're being watched."

Ethan nodded. "I understand that concern, but I want to make one thing clear: this isn't about micromanagement. It's about setting clear expectations and ensuring that we're all aligned—whether we're in the office or working remotely. We build accountability on trust. Without it, we risk losing the very foundation of what makes us successful."

Emma, the CTO, chimed in. "I think some of the resistance is also about transparency. People aren't used to having their work tracked so openly. It feels like everything is changing too fast for some, and they're feeling vulnerable. The changes have been especially challenging for those who've been here a long time and got used to doing things their own way under Victor and Jennifer."

"That's a good point," Ethan said. "But transparency is nonnegotiable. If we're going to repair our company's reputation successfully, everyone needs to be in alignment, and that means being open about our progress, challenges, and goals."

Leah, the VP of operations, shifted in her seat. "I agree with this point about transparency and accountability, but how do we balance that with giving managers the autonomy they need to lead their teams effectively?"

Ethan paused, considering his response. "It's about consistency. What we permit, we promote. If we allow certain teams or individuals to operate without clear accountability, we're promoting a culture of inconsistency. And that's where trust breaks down. But autonomy doesn't disappear with accountability. We're giving managers even more freedom to lead their teams, but with the understanding that there are clear expectations and measurable outcomes."

The tension in the room was palpable. Ethan scanned the faces of his executive team, noting the crossed arms, furrowed brows, and averted gazes. The latest debate over accountability and culture had once again reached a stalemate, with some executives clinging to the old ways of doing things.

Greg seemed to be the most disturbed. His usual affable geniality had disappeared. He had practically turned his whole body away from Ethan. "I just don't see how all this focus on culture is going to get us where we need to go. We've got deadlines, targets, and investors breathing down our necks. This feels like a distraction."

Ethan let Greg's words hang in the air for a moment before leaning forward, his hands clasped on the table in front of him. His voice was calm but carried an unmistakable edge of determination. "The board doesn't think it's a distraction. Actually, they're pleased with what we've done so far. They know it's the culture focus that's making it possible." He had just met with Tanya the previous Friday afternoon.

Samira spoke up. "I think we need to communicate this balance more clearly. Right now, some people feel like we're just imposing new rules without explaining the 'why.' We can be a lot more transparent with the reasoning behind these changes. We can show people that this isn't about controlling them. It's about making sure we're all moving in the same direction."

Ethan nodded, appreciating Samira's candor. "Yes. The 'why' behind these changes is crucial. It's not just about enforcing rules—it's about building trust and ensuring that everyone is contributing equally, no matter where they are. But let me be clear about something."

He leaned forward slightly, his tone taking on a sharper edge. "Every successful startup hits this point. The point where you have to decide: Are we going to double down on the way things were before—the way that led to crisis, burnout, turnover, and a fractured culture? Or are we going to treat our employees as a part of the solution?"

The room went silent. Even Greg seemed momentarily at a loss for words.

Ethan continued, his voice steady but growing in intensity. "We will not hit those targets, keep those clients, or satisfy those investors if our people don't trust us, if they don't feel like they're part of something bigger than a set of quarterly numbers. And that starts here, with us."

He leaned back slightly, giving the team a moment to absorb his words. "If we keep trying to fix today's problems with yesterday's mindset, we're going to lose. But if we're willing to lead differently—if we can show our teams that we value them not just as employees but as partners in this journey—that's how we win."

Ethan's gaze landed on Greg. "So, the question is, which path are we going to choose?" Ethan looked around the room, his voice softening. "We need to make sure that message is getting through, and it starts with us. Let's make this the moment we turn the page."

He stood up. "From now on, at every Monday meeting, we're going to review our progress on the four action steps. We're going to improve our communication, and we're going to double down on accountability. I'm betting that trust will follow."

THE BRIGHTPATH TOWN HALL
Trust and Communication

After the meeting, Ethan decided it was time to take a more direct approach with the staff. He scheduled a company-wide town hall meeting for that Thursday, intending to address the growing concerns head-on. The hybrid model could only work if everyone was on board, and that required not just enforcing accountability but also fostering trust through open communication.

Unfortunately, what Ethan had in mind was impossible to arrange within a week. He spent most of Tuesday ironing out the details with the board, and they insisted he postpone it to the following Thursday.

Thus, on Thursday morning, Ethan stood in front of a camera, ready to broadcast to Brightpath's global staff—those in the office and the remote teams tuning in from around the world. He had spent half of the previous day rehearsing this, with Samira as his presentation coach. Now his face appeared on the large screens scattered throughout the company's offices, and within moments, hundreds of employees were watching.

"Good morning, good afternoon, and good evening, everyone,

depending on your time zone," Ethan began, his voice calm but firm. "I want to take a few minutes to talk about the changes we've been making and why they're important. I know some of you have concerns about the new accountability measures, and I want to address those head-on."

He paused for a moment, letting his words sink in before he continued.

"First, let me make this clear: accountability is not about micromanagement. It's about trust. In a hybrid environment, where some of us are in the office and others are working remotely, it's easy for things to slip through the cracks. We need clear expectations and measurable outcomes to make sure that everyone, no matter where they're working, feels equally responsible for the company's success."

Ethan scanned the room in front of him, sensing the attentiveness of those watching. "But trust goes both ways. We're not implementing these measures to control anyone. We trust that each of you is here because you bring something valuable to this company. We are setting up a framework that allows us to collaborate more effectively, to communicate openly, and to hold ourselves accountable for the goals we've set together as a team."

He paused again, maintaining a connection with the employees watching remotely. "Change is hard, and it's understandable to have concerns or feel worried about the new rules that are being imposed for everyone. But this is about making Brightpath stronger. We aim to hear everyone's voice, and we value everyone's contributions, whether you're sitting in this office or working from your home halfway across the world."

The staff in the room he was in was silent, but he could feel the anticipation radiating through the screen.

"When I stepped into the role of CEO, I talked about trust, accountability, and transparent communication—principles I believe are vital to our success as a company. But principles only take us so far. To truly build a culture of collaboration and commitment, we need to go beyond words and put them into action."

Ethan paused for effect, his voice steady and clear.

"Today, on behalf of the Board of Directors, I'm announcing a company-wide equity grant for every single employee of Brightpath Solutions."

A ripple of stunned silence swept through the grid of faces, followed by visible excitement. "It happens right now for every employee here today. The forms are already on their way to you by email. For new employees joining us after today, the grant will be available after a year on the job. Yes, it means you all have stock in this privately held company—a small amount, because there are a lot of people here, but you'll all receive it in addition to your existing compensation."

Ethan continued, allowing a small smile to form. "This isn't just about recognition—it's about alignment. As shareholders, each of you will have a stake in Brightpath's success. Whether you're in the San Francisco office, working remotely, or collaborating from the other side of the globe, we are all part of this company's journey. We will all share the rewards of Brightpath's long-term success."

He took a breath, gauging the reactions on the screen. Some employees looked emotional; others were elated.

"Here's what this means: as we continue to grow, innovate, and overcome challenges, your contributions will directly affect not only our success but your own personal investment in this company. This equity grant, I hope, will foster a stronger sense of purpose and serve as a reminder that Brightpath's future depends on your hard work, creativity, and dedication."

A hand went up in the virtual chat, and Ethan nodded for the moderator to unmute the participant. A young woman from the product development team spoke, her voice slightly shaky.

"Ethan, this is… incredible. I've never worked anywhere that did something like this for employees. Thank you for believing in us."

Ethan smiled warmly. "It's not just belief—it's knowing. I've seen what this team is capable of. This is my way of ensuring that every one of you knows how valued you are. We're in this together."

He straightened his posture, his tone growing resolute.

"You used the word incredible, but in my view, every company should make a commitment like this to their employees. We need to grow our business back, and now you will see your own fortunes grow with it. Growth comes through innovation and customer experience, so that's where you would naturally put your energy. And that, in turn, will make the experience of working here, with like-minded people, something special."

Ethan had arranged for breakout groups that included both in-office employees and remote participants, ensuring everyone could collaborate seamlessly. These groups were organized to blend different locations and functions, promoting diverse perspectives. He then asked everyone to join their assigned groups and discuss what steps the company should take to rebuild itself and establish trust—in addition to the equity grant. What role would they each play? How could their team improve communication, accountability, and trust? He knew that it was not enough to tell them good news. He also had to listen.

As the breakout discussions wound down, Ethan watched the

participants filter back into the main session. Their energy was palpable, even through the screen. Several comments stuck in Ethan's mind:

- From a sales manager in San Francisco: "The equity grant is amazing, but what really struck our group was the symbolism of trust. We need to match that trust with our own openness—we each need to increase our willingness to be more direct about challenges we see with clients instead of sugarcoating things."

- From an engineering lead in Mumbai: "Now that we're all owners, I think we need a company-wide bug bounty program where we reward employees for finding bugs—not just for security issues, but for any inefficiency that costs us money."

- From a project coordinator in London: "We need a 'no acronym' policy in meetings. I've been here three years and still sometimes feel like people are speaking a different language."

- From a technical writer in San Francisco: "Maybe we could develop an internal 'tour of duty' program where people can temporarily try different roles—it might help us discover hidden talents."

- From a systems architect in Dubai: "Maybe we need designated 'devil's advocates' in planning meetings—people whose job it is to constructively challenge our assumptions."

- From a UX designer in Bangkok: "Our group focused on

communication transparency. We'd like to see more regular updates about company strategy and performance now that we're all shareholders."

- And from an HR specialist in Lagos: "This changes the way we think about our daily work. When you own a piece of the company, every improvement you make feels more meaningful."

As the comments continued, Ethan felt a growing sense of optimism. The town hall had transformed from a simple announcement into a foundation for deeper engagement and collaboration.

"This is just the beginning," he said. "From here on in, we're all accountable for our success. My role is to serve the company—and that means serving all of you. As we navigate the road ahead, let this grant be a symbol of our shared purpose and our commitment to each other. Together, we'll build something truly extraordinary."

A wave of applause spread over the room—both audible and visual as emojis flooded the chat. Ethan allowed himself a moment to soak it in. For the first time in weeks, he felt the weight on his shoulders lighten.

RECONNECTING WITH THE BOARD CHAIR

Trust, Trust, Trust

The town hall had the effect Ethan had hoped for. The initial resistance wasn't completely gone, but he could feel a shift in the atmosphere. His message about trust and accountability was resonating, and more importantly, employees were beginning to understand the "why" behind the changes.

But the actual test was yet to come. It would take time for these new expectations to become ingrained in Brightpath's culture. Some managers would adapt quickly, while others might struggle with the transition. Ethan knew he had to stay consistent, reinforcing the principles of trust and accountability every step of the way.

In the days following the town hall, Ethan checked in directly with managers and teams in Brightpath offices around the world. He visited some in person and convened other groups by video conferencing. He wanted to hear their concerns, address their questions, and double down on listening. Leading by example wasn't just about enforcing policies—it was about being present, about demonstrating the very trust and transparency he was promoting. Slowly but surely, the culture was shifting. Trust was being built, one brick at a time.

About two weeks after the town hall, he got an invitation from Tanya Grayson to meet her at her office in Palo Alto. Not a dinner in San Francisco. He immediately felt sheepish. He should have arranged a time with her immediately. After all, she had personally authorized the equity grant.

He thought about using a car service but decided to drive himself. Below the level of consciousness, he wanted some semblance of control over something—especially if the meeting went awkwardly.

The late afternoon sun cast long shadows through the windows of Tanya's building on Sand Hill Road. Ethan sat across from her, still energized from his two weeks of follow-up. "The response was incredible," he said. "People aren't just thinking about their own roles anymore—they're thinking about the whole company."

Tanya nodded her approval, her expression serious. "The equity grant was a bold move, Ethan. And yes, it's created momentum. I know the meeting went well. And the honeymoon. But now comes the hard part."

She stood and walked to the window, looking out over the Silicon Valley landscape where she'd watched countless companies rise and fall. "People are not telling you everything that's important," she said.

"How do you know that?"

"Because they never do." She turned and sat back down to face him, once again giving him the look of complete concentration, the look that said no one else mattered right now. "When companies recover from scandals—and I've seen quite a few try—there's a pattern. The initial changes create excitement and hope. But that's not enough. You have to turn that energy into sustained change."

"I know," Ethan said. "We need to—"

"Let me finish," Tanya interrupted. "Take Waste Management in the late 1990s. A new CEO comes in after an accounting scandal and makes big changes. Or, more recently, look at Zenefits. Both companies didn't just make symbolic changes—they rebuilt their entire operational framework." She paused. "The equity grant gives everyone skin in the game. But now they'll be watching every move you make, measuring whether their newfound ownership means anything real."

Ethan leaned forward. "So, what's your advice?"

"First, you need to systematize accountability," Tanya said, returning to her seat. "All those great ideas from the town hall? Create clear ownership and timelines for each initiative you pursue. When people own stock, they expect to see movement."

"We're already working on implementation teams—"

"Good. But that's just internal. We also need to think about our former clients." Tanya pulled out a tablet and opened a document. "I've been doing some research. Five major clients terminated their contracts during Victor's final months. Together, they represented almost 20 percent of our revenue."

Ethan nodded grimly. He knew the numbers all too well.

"Here's what's interesting," Tanya continued. "Three of them are still looking for solutions. They've tried other providers but haven't fully committed. That's our opening."

"You think they'd consider coming back? After everything that happened?"

"Companies can be surprisingly forgiving if you show them real change," Tanya said. "Look at what happened with Tyco after their scandal. They didn't just apologize—they demonstrated fundamental transformation in how they operated. That's what won back trust."

She slid the tablet across the desk. "I've made some initial contacts. Informally, through my network. Two CEOs are willing to have conversations—not with me, but with you."

Ethan studied the names on the screen. These were major players in their industry. Winning them back would be transformative for Brightpath. But it was all out of his comfort zone. As CHRO, he'd never dealt directly with clients.

"What's the approach?" he asked.

"Transparency," Tanya said firmly. "Complete transparency. Show them everything we're doing differently—the new accountability structures, the equity grant, the cultural transformation. But more importantly, demonstrate how these changes make us a better partner for them."

She leaned back in her chair. "But Ethan, here's what keeps me up at night. We're attempting something that hasn't really been done before. Yes, other companies have recovered from scandals. But promoting a CHRO to CEO? Building recovery around human-centered leadership at the scale of a whole company? That's new territory."

"It happens all the time at a smaller scale—for instance, in business units," Ethan said. "Don't you think it can happen here?"

Tanya smiled. "Of course I do. I think traditional recovery playbooks miss something crucial—the human element. Numbers matter, but trust matters more. You understand that better than any turnaround CEO I've backed. But precisely because we're charting new territory, we have to be flawless in our execution."

She stood again, this time moving to a whiteboard where she quickly wrote three terms, then pointed to each one as she said them: "Internal Trust, Client Trust, and Market Trust," then added vertical lines to create three columns.

"These are all interconnected," she said. "The equity grant builds internal trust. That should lead to better service, which rebuilds client trust. As clients return, market trust grows." She turned to face him. "But the chain is only as strong as its weakest link. We have to deliver on every front."

Ethan absorbed her words, feeling both the weight of the challenge and the clarity of the path forward. "We're going to make mistakes," he said finally.

"Of course we are," Tanya replied. "But if we're transparent about those mistakes, if we learn from them openly, that itself builds trust." She smiled. "You know, when I first suggested promoting you, some board members thought I was crazy. But I've watched too many companies try to recover through financial engineering alone. Numbers without trust are just another house of cards."

"I don't know these clients personally," Ethan said, studying the list. "How do I reach out to them?"

Tanya's eyes lit up, and Ethan recognized the energy that radiated from her whenever she shared especially hard-won wisdom.

"Start with Lisa Chen at Metro Industries. She's pragmatic, and she had a good relationship with Emma before everything went sideways. Have Emma reach out first—not to try to sell her, just to reconnect. Then you can send a short email acknowledging the past issues directly and requesting thirty minutes of Lisa's time."

Tanya pulled out her phone and began dictating: "Something like: 'I know Metro had concerns about Brightpath's leadership and transparency under the previous management. As the new CEO, I'd appreciate the opportunity to share how we're transforming our organization and hear your candid feedback about what we'd need to do to rebuild your trust.'"

She looked up at Ethan. "The key is that last part—you're not asking for them to come back to Brightpath. You're asking for their insight. People like Lisa have been in the industry for a long time. They have strong opinions about what makes a good technology partner. Give them the chance to share that wisdom."

"And the others?" Ethan asked.

"You'll need a different approach for Marcus at GlobalCorp," Tanya said. "He's all about innovation—that's why they left when our product roadmap stalled. Have Rajiv reach out first. Marcus respects him, and he'll be intrigued to hear that we promoted him to a global CFO role. Then you go in with a clear story about how our new structure is accelerating innovation." She paused. "But again, don't give him a sales pitch. Ask questions. Listen. They need to see that you aren't just a new CEO making promises—you'll need to convey to him that it's a fundamentally different Brightpath."

She erased the whiteboard. "Go win back those clients, Ethan. Show them what human-centered leadership really means. As I've said, if we can pull this off, we won't just save Brightpath—we'll create a new model for corporate recovery."

Driving back to the office, Ethan felt simultaneously sobered and energized. The equity grant wasn't an end point—it was barely the beginning. They would have to invent new ways of working, new approaches to accountability, and new methods of rebuilding trust. There was no playbook to follow because they were writing it as they went.

But maybe that was the point. In trying to rebuild Brightpath through trust, accountability, and communication, they had the chance to demonstrate a different way of doing business. As he pulled into his driveway back home, Ethan felt more certain than ever that they were on the right path.

LEADERSHIP TRAINING
Accountability

The day after his meeting with Tanya, Ethan had a scheduled one-on-one with Samira, the VP of HR. Samira was becoming his most valuable ally. She had helped to implement the new accountability measures, and she had brought the initial resistance of some of the managers to his attention. As Ethan entered her office, he could see that she had a lot on her mind.

"Hey, Samira. How's it going?" he asked as he took a seat across from her desk.

"Things are... progressing," she said with a cautious smile. "I think the town hall helped clarify a lot of the confusion, but we've still got some managers struggling with the balance between trust and accountability."

Ethan leaned forward. "What do you mean?"

Samira sighed. "There's this view among some managers that accountability means checking in on people constantly, but that's not what we're aiming for. We want accountability to come from a place of trust."

Ethan nodded. This was exactly what he'd been worried about.

"I think I see what you're saying," Ethan replied. "We need to make sure that trust goes beyond rhetoric and is demonstrated through each action and every task completed."

"Exactly," Samira said. "I think we need to reinforce that message, especially with the managers who are still adjusting."

Ethan leaned back, considering the best approach. "Let's organize some leadership training sessions. We'll focus specifically on how to build trust within teams and show that accountability is the natural result of that trust. I want to make sure our managers aren't just following orders—they need to internalize these values."

Samira smiled. "That's a good idea. I'll get started on the logistics. And Ethan, just so you know, I've also heard some positive feedback from team members who are seeing the benefits of these changes. It's slow, but it's happening."

Ethan smiled. "That's good to hear. Slow progress is still progress."

• • •

A few weeks later, Ethan stood in front of a small group of department heads for the first session of the leadership training. The room was a mix of in-office managers and virtual participants, their faces appearing on a large screen at the front of the room. The goal of the session was simple: to help Brightpath's leaders understand how to create the new atmosphere needed to inspire positive changes.

Ethan opened the session with a question. "How many of you feel like your teams trust you?" He scanned the room as a few hands tentatively rose. Some of the virtual participants responded with nods, but many were hesitant.

"That's what I thought," Ethan said. "And that's okay. Trust isn't something you get automatically when you become a leader. It's something you must earn. And if your team doesn't trust you, then everything else—communication, accountability, and collaboration—becomes a struggle."

He paused, letting the point settle in before he continued.

"I want you to think about trust like this: it's the foundation for everything we're trying to build. Without it, accountability feels forced. When your team trusts you, they'll naturally hold themselves accountable because they don't want to let you—or the rest of the team—down. But if there's no trust, they'll feel like accountability is really just micromanagement."

One manager, Claire, raised her hand. "So how do we build that trust, especially if we've been leading the same team for a while and they're used to a certain way of doing things?"

Ethan smiled. "That's a great question. The first step is transparency. Your team needs to know where you're coming from and why you're asking them to deliver certain results. They need to understand your intentions. If they feel you're holding them accountable just for the sake of metrics or control, they won't trust you. But if they see you're genuinely invested in their success, trust will follow."

Another manager chimed in from the virtual screen. "What about remote teams? It's harder to build trust when you're not interacting face-to-face."

"That's true," Ethan said. "But it's not impossible. Remote teams require even more communication than in-office teams. Regular check-ins, not just about work but about how they're doing personally, can go a long way. Find ways to demonstrate that you see them as people, not just employees working from home. And, again, be transparent. Remote workers can feel isolated, and if they don't know what's happening with the rest of the team, trust erodes quickly."

The session continued, with Ethan walking the managers through practical strategies for building trust, setting expectations, and creating environments where accountability was a natural result of strong relationships. By the end of the session, he felt confident the message was getting through.

That evening, as Ethan reviewed the day's progress, he received an email from Greg, the CCO.

> *Hey Ethan,*
>
> *Just wanted to share something. We've started doing those cross-team check-ins you suggested, and it's already making a difference. Remote workers are more engaged, and the in-office team is seeing them as part of the process, not just an afterthought. It's slow, but it's working.*
>
> *—Greg*

Ethan smiled as he read the message. This is such a great example of what it's all about—building trust, one step at a time. The culture at Brightpath was getting stronger, and while it wasn't an overnight transformation, he could see the seeds of a brighter and more successful path being planted.

• • •

Over the next few weeks, even as the audit process continued, the finance function began to experiment with new organizational approaches. Rajiv knew that by itself, their shared experience wouldn't bridge the deeper divide between the teams. Nor would process improvements do the trick; that was just the beginning. They needed to trust each other—not just as colleagues, but as partners working toward a shared goal.

He organized a series of informal virtual coffee chats, pairing team members from the two groups. These sessions had no set agenda, just a chance for people to share stories, interests, and experiences.

During one session, Priya shared how her team celebrated festivals like Diwali, while Mark talked about his passion for hiking in Colorado. Laughter filled the virtual room as they discovered surprising commonalities, like their shared love of spicy food.

Rajiv also arranged a cultural awareness workshop, where both teams learned about each other's work styles and communication preferences. The US team appreciated the opportunity to learn more about the India team's methodical approach, while the India team gained insight into the US team's expectations for quick turnaround times based on their more fast-paced work environment.

"It's funny," one US data analyst remarked after the session. "I always thought they were hesitant, but now I see they're just being thorough. It's something we could learn from."

The time spent learning about each other's culture and work style yielded results almost immediately. The India-based accounting team became more proactive in delivering reports ahead of deadlines, reducing the stress on the US finance team. In turn, the US team began to value the precision and dedication the India team brought to their work.

The new handoff system reduced delays, and the shared project tracker provided visibility across the board. Productivity soared, but more importantly, the tension between the teams dissolved.

Rajiv couldn't help but feel a sense of pride as he saw the transformation unfold. It wasn't just about fixing processes—it was about creating a culture of mutual respect and collaboration.

Late one evening, Rajiv sat at his desk, reviewing the latest financial report. The numbers were strong, but what pleased him most was the teamwork that had made it possible.

CLIENT OUTREACH
Trust and Accountability

During the next few weeks, Ethan continued to focus on reinforcing trust throughout the company. He intentionally contacted remote employees, ensuring they felt seen and valued. He encouraged managers to be transparent with their teams, explaining the reasons behind decisions and demonstrating that accountability wasn't about control—it was about mutual respect.

And slowly, the results were showing.

Teams were collaborating more openly. Remote employees were stepping up, feeling empowered to contribute fully. And the in-office teams were viewing their remote colleagues as equals, not just distant workers.

Ethan also began to lay the groundwork for reaching out to customers. First, he checked in with Greg, who would normally have this on his plate as CMO. Greg had been so busy with the internal reorganization of his four departments that he hadn't been able to pay much attention to client outreach. He responded with a little bit of reluctance to let go of one of his responsibilities, but he also understood the urgency. He also told Ethan that as CEO, his direct engagement would matter more than anything Greg could do.

Just as Tanya had predicted, Emma's initial reach-out to Lisa Chen opened the door. Within hours of Emma's casual message, Lisa had responded, expressing cautious interest in hearing about the changes at Brightpath. Ethan followed up with the exact email Tanya had suggested, and to his surprise, Lisa didn't wait to contact him until they had a scheduled meeting. She called him directly.

"I appreciate your message, Ethan," she said, her voice carrying both warmth and wariness. "Metro has a lot invested in Brightpath's architecture. Migrating away has been… challenging."

"I can imagine," Ethan replied, settling into the conversation. "And I suspect our lack of transparency during the transition didn't help."

There was a pause on the line. "No, it didn't," Lisa said finally. "But Emma tells me things are different now."

"They are. But rather than tell you about the changes we've made, I'd like to hear your perspective first. What would you need to see from us to consider rebuilding the relationship?"

What followed was a forty-five-minute conversation that reminded Ethan of his early meetings with Brightpath's employees. Lisa, like all the employees who were adjusting to the idea of a new CEO, needed someone to really listen. She outlined specific incidents where communication had broken down, where promises had been made and broken, and where trust had eroded in a series of small disappointments.

"The technology was never the issue," she explained. "It was the relationship. We never knew where we stood."

Ethan took notes throughout the call, and before they hung up, he read back the key points she'd raised. "So what I'm hearing is that you need three things: regular, scheduled check-ins with our technical teams, complete transparency about our development roadmap—including potential delays or changes—and a clear escalation path when issues arise. Is that accurate?"

"Yes," Lisa said, sounding slightly surprised at the precise summary. "But how can you ensure those things will happen?"

"Let me show you," Ethan said. He shared his screen and walked her through the new accountability systems they'd put in place—the same ones they were using internally. "Every commitment we make to you will be logged here, with clear ownership and timelines. You'll have access to this dashboard, and you'll see exactly who's responsible for each element of our relationship."

"That's... different," Lisa said slowly.

"We're also implementing something new," Ethan continued. "Every quarter, we want our key clients to rate us on trust metrics—not just technical performance. We're building this feedback directly into our team's goals and our company's KPIs." He also offered to assign the same teams to their account who they had worked with previously. That way, Metro would already be familiar with their Brightpath counterparts, and communication would be much easier.

By the end of the call, Lisa had agreed to a three-month trial renewal. "Start small," she said. "Let's rebuild this step-by-step."

Marcus at GlobalCorp posed a different challenge entirely. As Tanya had suggested, Rajiv made the first contact, and Marcus agreed to meet with Ethan. But where Lisa had been open to rebuilding, Marcus arrived with skepticism built up over months of frustration.

"Innovation isn't just about good ideas," he said in their first video call, his Singapore office visible in the background. "It's about consistent execution. Brightpath used to understand that."

"You're right," Ethan agreed, surprising Marcus with his directness. "We lost our way. But I'd like to show you how we're finding it again."

Instead of launching into a sales pitch, Ethan shared the employee equity grant story and the flood of innovation ideas that followed. He explained how they were systematically evaluating and implementing those ideas, using a new accountability framework the team developed.

Marcus listened politely but remained unconvinced. "Interesting approach," he said. "But GlobalCorp needs results, not experiments in corporate culture."

"Fair enough," Ethan replied. "So let me make you an unusual offer. Come visit our offices—any of them, on any day, without advance notice. Talk to our teams directly. See how we're working now. If you don't see concrete evidence of change, we'll cover all your expenses related to your visit and never bother you again."

The offer caught Marcus's attention. Two weeks later, he showed up unannounced at Brightpath's Mumbai office at nine o'clock in the morning local time. He spent the day moving between teams, asking pointed questions, and observing their processes. What he found was different from what he had expected.

The development teams showed him their new collaborative workflows, where customer feedback was integrated directly into the development process. He sat in on a team huddle where team members openly discussed challenges and collectively problem-solved. When he asked about recent failures, instead of deflection, he got honest analyses of what had gone wrong and what they'd learned.

"Your people are… enthusiastic," he told Ethan in their follow-up call. "But more importantly, they're aligned. Everyone I spoke to could explain not just what they were doing, but why it mattered to the bigger picture."

"That's what happens when people have real ownership," Ethan said. "Both literally, through equity, and figuratively, through trust and accountability."

Marcus nodded slowly. "I'm not ready to bring all our business back," he said. "But I'd be interested in exploring a pilot project. Something that would let us test this new Brightpath you're building."

THE QUALITY CRISIS

Communication and Accountability

Ethan didn't see it coming. Just when everything seemed to be falling into place—when the company's financial crisis had turned around, they had won back one of their three major clients, and trust and accountability were finally taking root at Brightpath—the Code Bright crisis hit. It began like many crises do: suddenly and without warning.

Late on a Friday afternoon, Leah, the VP of operations, called him. Her voice was tense, carrying an urgency Ethan hadn't heard in months.

"Ethan, we've got a serious problem," Leah said, her words clipped, as though she had rehearsed them but still struggled to say them out loud.

Ethan straightened in his chair, sensing the weight of what was coming. "Go on," he said, his heart rate quickening.

"The new software updates we've been rolling out to our top-tier clients—that Code Bright package that we prototyped?"

"Sure," Ethan said.

"It's crashing. And it's not just a few isolated incidents. We're getting reports from multiple clients, and some of them are threatening to pull their contracts if we don't fix this fast."

Ethan's stomach dropped. The software update had been one of their biggest initiatives, spearheaded by Emma's tech team. It was supposed to boost Brightpath's revenue growth and help them secure long-term contracts. But now, instead of cementing the company's position as an industry leader, it was spiraling into a full-blown disaster.

"I'll call an emergency meeting right away," Ethan said to Leah, standing from his desk. "Get Emma and Greg on the line. We need to contain this before it spreads any further."

Within thirty minutes, Ethan had gathered the executive team in the conference room. Emma was already on the screen from London, looking tense and tired. Greg sat across from Ethan, his phone buzzing with messages from the marketing teams, who were getting bombarded by client complaints.

Ethan opened the meeting, his voice steady but his tone urgent. "We've got multiple reports of the software update crashing at key client sites. Some clients are threatening to pull contracts if this isn't fixed immediately. Emma, what's the status?"

Emma, visibly stressed, took a deep breath. "We've identified the root cause, but it's going to take time to implement the fix. It's going to take at least forty-eight hours to get a stable patch out, and that's if everything goes smoothly."

Greg, clearly frustrated, jumped in. "Honestly, Ethan, I'm not sure Emma's team can handle this on their own. We've had issues with tech before, and now it's costing us some of our biggest clients. I think we need to bring in outside help to make sure this gets done right."

The room fell silent.

Emma's face tightened on the screen, clearly taken aback, but before she could respond, Ethan raised a hand to interrupt. He looked directly at Greg, his voice calm but firm. Everyone in the room had been shaken by Greg's tone. It was undermining the open and collaborative environment they were trying to cultivate, and Ethan felt it was essential to address it immediately.

"I understand your frustration, Greg," Ethan said. "We're all feeling the pressure. But blaming each other will not solve this. Emma's team is already working around the clock to fix the issue, and I trust them to get it done."

Greg shifted in his seat, his dissatisfaction clear. "I'm just saying we can't afford any more mistakes. This is a huge issue, especially coming after the Victor fiasco. We need to make sure we're bringing in the right expertise if things don't go smoothly."

Ethan paused a moment to let everyone settle down before speaking again. "You're right, Greg. We can't afford any more mistakes. But trust goes both ways. We've spent months building a culture based on trusting each other to deliver, and I will not throw that away the moment things get tough. Emma's team is capable, and they've shown repeatedly that they can step up when it matters."

He turned to address the rest of the team. "We've built this company on the principles of trust and accountability. That means when things go wrong, we don't point fingers—we work together to fix the problem. I trust all of you to do your part to make sure we get through this."

Ethan's words hung in the air for a moment before Leah, the VP of operations, spoke up. "I agree with Ethan. Emma's team has always delivered under pressure, and I don't think now's the time to second-guess them. Let's focus on getting the patch out and keeping our clients informed."

Rajiv, the CFO, chimed in from the video screen. "From a financial perspective, we need to reassure our clients as quickly as possible. Greg, if your team can draft the message, I'll work with you to make sure it aligns with our numbers and projections."

"We also need to make sure we're on top of the issue," Leah said. "We should have someone on-site at every major client's office, pulling data, keeping in touch with Emma's team, and getting ready to reinstall."

Greg finally nodded, still looking tense but more aligned with the plan. "Alright, I'll get the message out. But we need to be sure the patch is solid before we communicate any timelines."

Ethan turned back to Emma. "Emma, I know you're working around the clock on this, but I need you to keep me updated every step of the way. The moment we hit any delays or roadblocks, I want to know. We can't afford any surprises here."

Emma, looking relieved, nodded. "I'll keep you informed. I've already got the development team working on the patch. They're pulling an all-nighter to get this done."

* * *

The next forty-eight hours were a whirlwind. Ethan barely left the office, coordinating with the executive team to manage the fallout. Every few hours, he checked in with Emma's team to monitor the progress of the patch. Meanwhile, Greg's marketing teams worked tirelessly to reassure clients and keep them updated on Brightpath's commitment to resolving the issue.

But the pressure was mounting. By Sunday afternoon, Ethan received a call from one of Brightpath's largest clients.

"Ethan, we've been a loyal customer for years, but this is unacceptable," the client said, frustration clear in their voice. "If this doesn't get resolved soon, we'll have no choice but to look elsewhere."

Ethan listened calmly, fully aware of the stakes. "I understand your frustration, and I take full responsibility for this. Our team is working around the clock to resolve the issue, and I assure you we'll have a fix by tomorrow morning. We value your partnership, and we'll make this right."

"I'd feel a lot better if—" the client began.

"I know," Ethan said. "If Victor were here. However, in light of what we now know, it's good that he's not. You saw us move quickly as soon as the information about what he was up to came to light. We were up and running within a few days. We take this just as seriously—even more so."

...

By Sunday night, the patch was finally ready for release. Emma's team had pulled off what seemed impossible, fixing the issue faster than anyone had expected. The relief in the room was palpable when Emma confirmed the deployment.

"The patch is live," she announced over the video call. "We've already had confirmation from a few clients that the crashes have stopped."

Ethan let out a breath he didn't realize he'd been holding. "Thank you, Emma. You and your team did an incredible job under pressure." But the work wasn't over yet. "Greg, I want you to follow up personally with every major client affected. Let them know we've fixed the issue and offer any additional support they might need. We need to repair the relationships that were damaged during this crisis."

Greg nodded, already sending messages to his team.

Ethan closed his laptop, feeling the exhaustion settle over him. They had averted the crisis, but it revealed just how vulnerable Brightpath still was. One major issue could have unraveled all the time and effort they'd spent on their recovery.

More than that, the crisis had tested their new approach to leadership. Ethan had relied on the trust they had built internally to navigate the chaos. Emma's team had delivered under extreme pressure, and Greg's team had maintained transparency with their clients throughout the ordeal. Without that foundation of trust, things could have easily fallen apart.

HIGH PERFORMANCE
Accountability and Trust

On Monday morning, as Ethan reviewed the final reports from the crisis, he felt a mixture of relief and resolve. They had tested the trust they built, and it endured. Clients had responded positively. Some said their opinion of Brightpath was better—now that they'd seen the company, guided by its new executive team, handle two crises in a row. Even the board seemed unruffled. Tanya had sent Ethan an email with just two words: *Nicely done*.

But now came the real challenge—turning this near-disaster into a lesson that would strengthen Brightpath.

In next Monday's executive meeting, he tried to highlight the resilience they had shown.

"We made it through this crisis because we've built something stronger than just a business—we've built a culture of trust," Ethan said. "But this was a wake-up call. We can't let our guard down. We need to continue reinforcing that trust, both internally and with our clients. The next time something like this happens—and there will be a next time—we'll be even better prepared."

Emma, Greg, and the rest of the team nodded in agreement. They had survived the storm, but Ethan knew that true leadership wasn't about surviving one crisis. It was about using that crisis to build something even stronger.

"We've made tremendous progress on the culture front," Ethan said. "The revelations about what Victor was really up to got people's attention. The equity grants reassured them that we were on their side. Setting new performance targets has shown that we believe in our own abilities."

He paused for emphasis. "But it's the more effective communications, accountability, and trust work that made the most difference. We're seeing it in the way we behave. The divide between remote and in-office teams is shrinking. Our time to market is faster—look how fast you and your team turned around the upgrade, Emma. I can see signs that trust is growing—for instance, the way we talk here. And as you know, at least two of the clients we lost are coming back, and we're signing up new clients, too. Thanks, Greg. Thanks, everyone."

"There are still a few fixes to be done," Emma said.

"But that's to be expected, and the additional fixes are adding to our credibility—not reducing it," said Ethan. "And that leads to the next point. We need to boost our performance. Some of the investors are feeling uneasy, and it is vital we show them that the changes we've made are translating into results."

Greg leaned forward in his chair, looking skeptical. "I get that we have to increase performance, Ethan, but are we sure the cultural changes haven't slowed us down? I'm hearing from my team that all these extra check-ins and trust-building exercises are taking time away from getting actual work done."

Ethan had been expecting this pushback. Greg had always been results-driven, but lately, his resistance to the company's new direction was becoming more apparent.

"I hear your concerns, Greg," Ethan said calmly. "But without trust, we wouldn't have been able to get through either one of these crises. It's not about slowing down—it's about making sure we're aligned and working together. Building a strong culture ensures we're all pulling in the same direction. We won't waste as much time and effort second-guessing each other."

Greg frowned, clearly unconvinced. "I just don't want us to lose focus. Results matter most. We can't get distracted by this 'soft stuff.'"

Ethan felt the tension in the room. The rest of the team was watching, waiting to see how he would respond.

"I agree results are crucial," Ethan said, while he maintained his composure. "But the results won't be consistent if our foundation isn't strong. Under Victor, the lack of trust and accountability was affecting morale and creating communication breakdowns. We need both—a strong culture and powerful performance. They're not mutually exclusive."

Leah, the VP of operations, nodded in agreement. "I think the changes are helping. We're more efficient because people trust each other. And there's a lot more we can do in terms of reducing unnecessary work. When you have an atmosphere of trust, you don't need nearly as much oversight."

Rajiv added, "We've got the foundation. If we execute on performance with the same dedication we've shown to improving our culture, we'll be fine."

Greg remained unconvinced. "Alright," he said, leaning back in his chair. "But we need to keep our eye on the results. That's what will keep this company afloat."

• • •

Over the next few weeks, the push for performance began in earnest. Ethan worked closely with his executive team to set clear, ambitious goals for each department. The focus was on growth—new client acquisition, improved efficiency, and boosting revenue. But the underlying message remained the same: trust first, accountability second, and both held together with transparent and direct communication.

Ethan stayed visible throughout the process. He scheduled more frequent check-ins with department heads to reinforce that he wasn't just pushing for results—he was there to support them.

Most of the team responded well to the increased pressure. Emma's tech team continued to optimize product development processes, speeding up delivery times without compromising quality. Leah's operations team tightened up on internal processes, cutting waste and improving efficiency across the board.

But Ethan noticed Greg was becoming more distant. While his marketing teams were delivering results, there were signs that Greg was pushing them harder than necessary, focusing solely on numbers without promoting the collaborative culture Ethan had been working to build.

• • •

One afternoon, Ethan scheduled a check-in with Greg to discuss his concerns.

"Greg, I've been noticing some tension in your department," Ethan began. "Your team is delivering, but I'm hearing that the pressure is wearing on them."

Greg didn't hesitate to respond. "Look, Ethan, we're in a critical time. We're still rushing to meet our client acquisition targets, and we can't afford to relax. My team knows we must deliver—if that means pushing them hard, so be it."

Ethan frowned. "Pushing for results is one thing, but we need to balance that with ways to support the culture we've built. If we lose the trust and collaboration that's been driving our success, we'll burn people out."

Greg shrugged. "I get it, but I'm focused on hitting those targets. Everything else is secondary right now."

Ethan paused, contemplating his next words. "Greg, I value your contributions, but we can't lose sight of the bigger picture. The results matter but so does how we achieve them. The 'how' matters just as much as the 'what.' If we undermine the culture we've built, the results won't be sustainable."

But Ethan knew Greg wasn't really on board. The growing disconnect was clear.

As the weeks went on, Greg's resistance became more pronounced. While his team continued to perform, the signs of strain were showing. Greg was a powerful performer, but his resistance to the company's culture and his refusal to align with the leadership vision was becoming toxic. Something would have to give.

THE BURNOUT LEADER

Accountability

Ethan sat in his office; the glow of his computer screens was the only light in the room. Ethan had Rajiv's financial reports spread out before him; they showed solid numbers—growth, increased revenue, and higher client retention rates. But despite the positive metrics, a knot of anxiety twisted in Ethan's gut. Greg's department, though delivering the strongest numbers, was setting off alarm bells in other ways.

People were dropping more and more hints. There were hushed conversations about overwork, complaints about late-night deadlines, and whispers about being pushed too far. Marketing staff were beginning to refer to Greg as TBL, for "the burnout leader." Greg's relentless pursuit of numbers had brought success, but at what cost? There had been a spike in transfer requests out of his department, a clear sign people were looking for an escape.

Ethan took a deep breath, his fingers tapping idly on his desk. Firing a top performer—especially one who had delivered through crises—was risky. But keeping Greg meant letting toxic leadership fester. Ethan knew he had to confront Greg, but this wasn't just about a performance review. It was about safeguarding the company's culture, a culture they had worked so hard to build.

Ethan leaned back in his chair, rubbing his temples. The glow of his laptop illuminated the room, but he barely noticed it. The day had been long, and although he'd made progress, the resistance wore on him.

A knock at the door broke his thoughts.

"Come in," he said, straightening his posture.

The door opened to reveal Tanya Grayson, the board chair, in one of her customary tailored suits.

"This is a pleasant surprise," Ethan said, starting to stand up. Tanya stopped him with a wave of her hand. "What brings you up here to the city so late?" It was the first time she had ever visited him at Brightpath's offices.

Tanya stepped into the room as she turned on the light, her expression kind but serious. "I had to come up here for a dinner," she said, "and I thought I'd check in on you. I know these last few weeks haven't been easy."

Ethan gestured toward the chairs across from his desk. "Please, have a seat."

Tanya settled into the chair with her hands clasped on her lap. "Ethan, I've been in your shoes more times than I care to admit. Leading through cultural change isn't for the faint of heart. It's messy, uncomfortable, and it feels like you're pushing a boulder uphill."

Ethan nodded, his shoulders relaxing slightly. "That's exactly how it feels. I know we're making progress, but there are moments when I wonder if I'm asking for too much, too fast."

Tanya leaned forward, her gaze steady. "You're not. It got you to this point. You did well in the crisis—in both crises. The changes you're driving—trust, accountability, transparency—are the foundation of any lasting success for Brightpath. Without them, everything else crumbles, no matter how strong the numbers look on paper."

Ethan exhaled, grateful for the support. "It's just... not everyone sees it that way. Greg, for one, is pushing back hard. He thinks all this focus on culture is a distraction from performance."

Tanya chuckled softly. "There's always a Greg. I've worked with plenty of leaders like him—results-driven to a fault. And you know what? They burn bright, but they burn out fast. If you only chase numbers, you lose sight of the people who deliver them. Trust me, Ethan. The approach you're taking will outlast any quarterly report."

Ethan allowed a small smile to tug at the corner of his mouth. "That's reassuring to hear."

Tanya nodded. "It's the truth. And I'll tell you something else—I've seen what happens when leaders abandon the values they're trying to build. It's chaos. You're on the right path, even if it doesn't always feel that way."

Ethan leaned back, his confidence restored. "Thank you, Tanya." Then his eyes narrowed. "You knew about Greg, didn't you?"

Tanya winked at him, got up, and started to move out of the office. "You're doing good work, Ethan. Don't lose sight of that. And don't let the Gregs of the world get you down."

As Tanya left the room, Ethan sat back down, a renewed sense of purpose settling over him. He still had a long road ahead, but knowing he had the chairperson's support made the climb feel a little less steep.

THE ULTIMATUM

Accountability

The next morning, the Ethan and Greg had their regular weekly meeting scheduled. Greg entered Ethan's office with a confident stride, as if the conversation were merely a formality. He sat down and crossed his arms, his demeanor exuding an air of impatience. He didn't wait for Ethan to begin.

"Ethan, I've just reviewed the numbers. We're hitting every target. Our team's performing better than ever despite the pressure. Is there a problem?" Greg asked, his tone more defensive than inquisitive.

Ethan clasped his hands in front of him, taking a moment before speaking. "Greg, I won't deny that your team is delivering results. And we need them. But I've been hearing growing concerns, too. The pressure is intense, and people are burning out. They feel like they're being pushed beyond their limits."

Greg didn't flinch. Instead, he leaned forward, his eyes narrowing. "That's part of the job, Ethan. We can't hit these numbers without pushing people. Everyone knows what's at stake."

Ethan sat back, studying Greg's posture. His words "part of the job" echoed in his mind. This was the difference of opinion. Greg didn't understand—or didn't want to understand—that there was more to leadership than just hitting numbers.

"I understand the pressure we're under," Ethan said calmly. "But what you're doing is unsustainable. The team is exhausted, and they're fracturing. We've had multiple transfer requests out of your department in the last month alone."

Greg shrugged dismissively. "Those are just people who can't handle the heat. We'll replace them if we need to."

Ethan felt a flash of frustration but quickly contained it. Greg wasn't just indifferent to the team's well-being; he was blind to the long-term consequences of his approach.

"That's exactly the problem, Greg," Ethan said, his voice firm but measured. "We can't just replace people every time they burn out. Brightpath isn't just about short-term results—it's about building something sustainable. Our culture is our competitive edge. If we lose that, the numbers won't matter in the long run."

Greg shifted in his seat, clearly irritated. "Look, Ethan, we don't have the luxury of slowing down."

Ethan nodded slowly, choosing his words carefully. "I get that, Greg. There are consequences if we miss our targets. But there are other ways to reach them. And there are consequences if people get frustrated. If they lose their trust in you, then we won't make our targets anyway—not the ones that matter most."

Greg's face tightened. "So, what are you saying? That we should prioritize their comfort over performance? That's not how business works, and you know it."

Ethan's jaw clenched. This was the crux of it. Greg was unable or unwilling to see the bigger picture. It wasn't about comfort or results.

Brightpath's foundation of trust, accountability, and communication—the very things that were now driving its success—were being systematically eroded by Greg.

"I'm saying that if we don't take care of our people, we'll lose them," Ethan said, his voice growing firmer. "And if we lose them, we lose the company. Short-term wins won't sustain us if we burn through our talent."

Greg crossed his arms, leaning back in his chair. "So, what's the solution, Ethan? You want me to ease up? Should we lower our expectations? Because if that's what you're asking, we'll lose out to competitors who don't."

Ethan shook his head, frustration creeping into his tone. "You can push people without breaking them. Right now, you're burning them out, and that's not leadership—it's destruction."

For a moment, silence hung between them. Ethan could see the stubbornness in Greg's eyes, the refusal to admit that his way wasn't working. It was a familiar pattern—Greg's focus on results at the expense of everything else. And yet, as much as Ethan wanted to help Greg see the value of sustainable leadership, he knew it was too late.

He leaned forward, meeting Greg's eyes directly. "So now you have a decision to make. Do you want to stay at Brightpath and align with the values we've worked hard to establish? Or do you want to leave? Because the way things are going right now, something must change."

Greg straightened in his chair, his tone growing icy. "So, what are you saying, Ethan? You're going to fire me for getting results? For doing what's necessary?"

Ethan took a deep breath, his decision clear in his mind. "Yes, Greg. I am."

Greg blinked, stunned for a moment, before anger flashed across his face. "You're making a mistake, Ethan. I've kept this company afloat. If you think you can hit these targets without me, you're in for a rude awakening."

Ethan remained calm, though he could feel the tension rising. "Greg, you've done a lot for this company, but your leadership style is toxic. It's not sustainable, and it's costing us more than just performance. We need leaders who can drive results *and* maintain the culture we've built."

He forced himself to take a breath. The next words were the most difficult he could remember having to say. "So, no, I'm not responding to your ultimatum. I don't believe it's accurate. You should pack up and go."

Greg stood abruptly, his chair scraping loudly against the floor. "You'll regret this," he spat before storming out, slamming the door behind him.

• • •

The silence in the office was deafening after Greg's departure. Ethan exhaled slowly, the gravity of what had just happened settling over him. Firing a top performer like Greg wasn't a decision he had made lightly, but he knew it was the right one. Trust and accountability weren't just words—they were the foundation of everything the company stood for.

For a moment, Ethan felt the weight of his decision bearing down on him. He knew Greg would stir up noise on his way out. It would cause ripples across the company. But he also knew that allowing Greg to stay would have caused deeper, more destructive consequences in the long term.

Ethan stood up and walked over to the window, gazing out at

the city skyline. The sun was setting, casting a golden glow over the buildings. The door to his office creaked open, and Leah, the VP of operations, stepped inside, her expression tentative.

"Ethan, I heard about Greg," she whispered.

Ethan turned to face her, nodding. "Yeah, I just let him go."

Leah crossed the room and sat down, her brow furrowed. "I think it was the right call. The way he's been driving his team—it was getting out of control. People were afraid to speak up, but everybody knew."

Ethan rubbed the back of his neck, feeling the fatigue setting in. "It wasn't easy. But we've built this company's culture based on trust, and I'm not willing to let that slip—even if it means making hard choices."

Leah stood and gave him a reassuring nod. "The team will understand. They trust you."

After she left, Ethan sat down at his desk once more, the weight of the day still pressing on him. It wasn't just about Greg. This was about the kind of company Brightpath would become—the kind of leader Ethan wanted to be. He had made a tough decision today, but Brightpath's future depended on people's trust in their leaders.

He stepped into the reception area. "Andrea? Please get Tanya Grayson on the line."

THE MARKETING STORY
Communication and Accountability

The day after Greg's departure, word spread quickly. Ethan walked into the office, knowing he had to address the team. It wasn't just about explaining why Greg was gone. It was about reinforcing the values that had led to the decision. The company was at a crossroads, and Ethan needed to make sure they continued moving forward.

By mid-morning, Ethan had gathered the executive team for a quick impromptu meeting. "I'm sure you've all heard by now that Greg is no longer with the company," he began, keeping his tone measured. "This was not a simple decision, but it was a necessary one. Greg was a strong performer, but the way he was leading his team was not in line with the values we're building here at Brightpath." He explained that he had asked Greg if he could accept the new values and that Greg fundamentally believed they were harming performance. "It's not that he refused to change his approach," Ethan said. "It's that he couldn't. In that respect, he was honest. I fired him on the spot. It was an extremely painful thing to do, and I haven't spoken to him since. I'm sure he sees this as unfair and misguided. He said I was 'firing him for good performance.' But after some reflection, I'm convinced it was the right choice. He was in charge of marketing, sales, customer service, client outreach, and public relations. These teams are all incredibly important for Brightpath right now. If we aren't living our values, messages will get to our customers that will not feel authentic."

Leah, the VP of operations, nodded. "I think everyone could see the tension building in his department. It was getting harder to manage."

Rajiv, the CFO, spoke next. "I think you made the right call, Ethan. Greg was delivering, but it was becoming clear that he was doing more harm than good in the long run. We've seen the strain in other departments as well."

Emma, the CTO, was more reflective. "It's always tough when someone like Greg leaves, especially because he was such a public face for the company. But I think this will ultimately send the right message—that how we treat each other matters just as much as the results we deliver."

Ethan took a deep breath. "I want to be clear that this isn't just about performance—it's about the culture we've built. We've worked hard to create an environment of trust, communication, and accountability. And that can't be compromised, even by someone who's delivering results."

Everyone on the team nodded, and Ethan could sense that they understood the gravity of the decision.

"I want each of you to communicate this to your teams," Ethan continued. "Let them know that while we value performance, we value how we achieve those results even more. And let's make sure that Greg's departure is seen as an opportunity for us to reinforce the principles that have gotten us this far."

• • •

Later that afternoon, Ethan called an emergency company-wide town hall to address the transition with the entire organization. This meeting was completely virtual. Even the employees in the San Francisco office would join from their computers at their desks. He knew there were questions, and he wanted to answer them quickly and head-on.

As the screen flickered to life and faces from offices and home offices around the world appeared, Ethan took a moment to gather his thoughts before speaking.

"Good morning, good afternoon, and good evening, everyone. I wanted to talk about the changes happening here at Brightpath and what they mean for all of us," Ethan began. "By now, many of you know our chief marketing officer"—and he gave Greg's full name—"is no longer with the company. I know this is shocking news for some, but I want to explain the reasons behind this decision."

Ethan paused, making sure the room was with him before he continued. "Greg was an incredibly strong performer, and his contributions to Brightpath were significant. But as I've said many times before, it's not just about what we achieve—it's about how we achieve it. Over the past few months, we've seen an increasing disconnect between how Greg was leading his team and the values we've been working to instill as a company."

He glanced at the screen, seeing nods of understanding from the faces looking back at him.

"I'm going to have to digress for a minute," Ethan said, "and explain how we will talk about this with the outside world. This includes any questions you get from the press, as well as what to share with family and friends. Like it or not, because of our ongoing story about Victor and our recovery, Brightpath is a highly visible company. Fortunately, it's visible for good reasons now—because we're trying to live our values and practice what we preach. We can't speak for Greg, and you shouldn't try to, but his departure stemmed from philosophical differences."

"If the press contacts you," Ethan continued, "you are trusted to communicate. Most companies would forbid employees from talking with reporters at all. But we're building an atmosphere of trust. At the same time, remember the commitment we've all made to the future of this company." He told them that they had all been sent a fact sheet with talking points, as well as Andrea's email address. They could forward her any press, comment, or social media requests, no matter how big or small.

"We said we believe in leading with trust, accountability, and respect," Ethan concluded. "We said we believe in building each other up, not pushing each other to the breaking point. And this episode became a test of our beliefs. While Greg was delivering results, the way those results were being achieved was not sustainable. It was eroding the trust and culture that have been so important to our success."

Ethan let his words settle before he continued. "This decision wasn't easy, but it was necessary to protect the long-term health of our company. I want us to remember why we're here. It's not just about the numbers—it's about the people. The relationships we build and the trust we create will drive our success far more than any single metric."

The room was silent for a moment before someone spoke up. "Thank you, Ethan. I think we all needed to hear that."

Ethan smiled, feeling a sense of relief. The message was received, and it was time to move forward.

• • •

In the days following the town hall, Ethan noticed a shift in the company's atmosphere. The tension from Greg's departure had started to lift, and in its place was a renewed sense of focus. Teams seemed more aligned, and the collaboration between departments felt smoother.

Emma's engineering team, once frustrated by Greg's constant pressure, seemed more energized. Marketing, which had been under intense strain, was finding its rhythm again, with more open communication and less fear of failure. Leah's operations team was already reporting improved morale.

But Ethan knew that the transition wouldn't be without its challenges. Greg had been a key figure in the company, and his departure left a significant gap. The search for a new CMO would take time, and in the interim, Ethan had to step in and provide support where needed. He found mid-level leaders in the department to handle customer service, sales, and PR, each with the skills and potential to stabilize their respective areas. However, when it came to the broader oversight of the department, there was a glaring gap: no one stood out as ready to step into the role of CMO.

Greg had not taken the time to develop or mentor potential successors, leaving the department vulnerable and overly reliant on his leadership. Ethan realized this lack of preparation reflected poorly on Greg's approach to leadership. A true leader not only delivers results but also ensures the team can thrive in their absence. This failure underscored the importance of building a leadership pipeline.

With no immediate candidate to step into Greg's shoes, Ethan decided that he would temporarily take on the responsibilities of the CMO himself. By doing so, he could ensure continuity in the department while simultaneously assessing the talent within the team to identify who might be ready for future leadership development. While a significant commitment of time and focus, Ethan viewed it as an opportunity to stabilize the department and cultivate a stronger foundation for the future.

He would also put his energy into recruiting the new marketing leader. Finding the right person to step into Greg's shoes would be critical to maintaining the momentum they had built.

MARKETING BETWEEN LEADERS

Communication, Trust

Ethan knew Greg's departments would feel the aftershocks of losing their high-profile leader. The day after Greg's exit, Ethan made a point of visiting the floor where Greg's office used to be. People were busy at their desks, but many of them quickly gathered around him in the break room. They simply wanted to talk through their experiences.

He noticed a sharp sense of organizational vertigo. Yesterday, they had been driven by hard deadlines and constant pressure. Today, they weren't sure what to do next. Some were clearly loyal to Greg's results-oriented approach, while others seemed relieved to have the pressure lifted.

The team needed a new leader—someone who could push them toward success without sacrificing the values of trust and collaboration. But before that, they needed stability.

Ethan gathered Greg's whole team in the conference room, which included about thirty people in the office and another forty-five remote employees joining via Zoom. He opened the meeting with a simple message. "I know the last few weeks have been challenging, but I want you all to know that we're moving forward together. This isn't about the past—it's about what comes next."

He looked around the room, taking in the expressions on the faces of those who had been under Greg's leadership. Some people looked relieved, while others were frowning or biting their lips.

"I realize that Greg's departure was sudden, but it was also a long time coming. There was an ongoing conflict over his choice of leadership style. He and I both realized that this high-pressure approach doesn't fit with the way we do things anymore. When I made the decision to let him go, I did it with the long-term health of the company in mind. But we both took part in it. It happened during a conversation between us."

There was a discernible gasp. *Oh well,* Ethan thought. *That's what happens when you choose to create a culture of trust and transparency.*

"You've all done incredible work," he continued, "and that doesn't go unnoticed. But I also want to be clear. Going forward, we'll do things differently from the way Greg did them. We're not just focused on hitting numbers. We're focused on how we get there, and that means building on the trust and collaboration that makes Brightpath what it is."

The team seemed to absorb his words, and Ethan sensed a shift in the atmosphere. The tension that had been present under Greg's leadership was lifting.

When Ethan paused, he was not surprised that an employee asked the question on everyone's mind, "Who will replace Greg?"

"We are looking outside the firm," Ethan said. "We want somebody who can help us build a whole new growth strategy, with social media skills to match. We're certainly open to suggestions for candidates.

Meanwhile, we're appointing employees from within to lead sales, customer service, marketing, and PR. We'll announce those names very shortly."

As soon as he finished speaking, many people put their hands up to ask follow-up questions. There were so many unsettled details. Many employees in the department were anxious and wanted to know more. Ethan called on one of the many people with their hands still raised. Their question was on the minds of many in the room, as well as all the remote team members. "And what will happen in the meantime?"

"We're figuring that out, too," Ethan said. "For the moment, I'll step in to handle the current major issues, including outreach on our two major news events—now three—if you count Greg's departure."

Later that afternoon, Ethan met with Emma and Leah to discuss how they could support the marketing team during the leadership transition.

"I think we need to give them some breathing room," Emma said. "They've been under a lot of pressure, and while their performance numbers are still high, we need to make sure we don't push too hard right now."

Leah nodded in agreement. "Agreed. We can't afford to lose momentum, but we need to rebuild trust within that team. Greg's departure was a signal that things are changing, and we need to make sure they know they've got our support."

Ethan leaned back in his chair, considering their input. "You're both right. The last thing we want is for the team to feel like they're being left to fend for themselves. Let's focus on stabilizing things for now. I'll check in with the department heads to make sure we're staying on track without overloading them."

They set the plan for the next few weeks; Ethan would step in to support the marketing teams until they found Greg's replacement. It wouldn't be easy, but it was necessary to ensure the company stayed aligned with its values while maintaining performance levels.

In addition, Ethan remained directly involved with the rehabilitation of client relationships for the companies that left when Victor was fired. He felt especially good about Metro Industries, which quickly integrated into Brightpath's new systems. They expressed keen interest in the trust leadership training, and Brightpath even piloted a version of it, integrated with the technological change training. Metro's CEO, Lisa, continued to work with Emma on joint pilots and initiatives.

Marcus at GlobalCorp took longer to convince. The pilot project he proposed was challenging—exactly the kind of innovative work that had stalled under the previous contract. But now, with clearer communication channels and stronger accountability, the Brightpath teams had risen to the challenge. What impressed Marcus most was not that everything went smoothly—it didn't—but he appreciated being kept informed and was pleasantly surprised at how well Brightpath handled the bumps.

"You promised transparency," he told Ethan and Emma during a review meeting. "I have to admit, I didn't expect you to be quite this transparent about the problems you're encountering."

"Problems are opportunities to build trust," Ethan replied, echoing what he'd been telling his teams. "We'd rather share a challenge early and work through it together than hide it and lose your trust later."

By the end of the quarter, Metro had fully renewed their contract with an expanded scope. GlobalCorp's pilot was showing promising results, and Marcus was beginning to discuss broader implementation. More importantly, both companies were serving as references for other former clients who were watching Brightpath's transformation with interest.

• • •

Reporting back to Tanya, Ethan reflected on the parallels between rebuilding employee trust and client trust. "It's the same principles," he said. "Be candid about where you are and where you're going. Create clear accountability for every commitment. Invite people to engage rather than try to sell them something. And most importantly, show them through actions, not just words, that you're serious about change."

Tanya smiled. "You're learning," she said. "But here's what's really interesting—you're not just rebuilding client relationships. You're creating a new kind of client partnership, one based on the same principles of trust and accountability that you're using internally. That's much harder to compete with than just having good technology."

Ethan nodded, thinking about the dozens of small interactions that had gone into rebuilding these two key relationships. It wasn't always easy, and they were still learning and had to stay on their toes to continue refining and adapting their approaches. But with each honest conversation, each fulfilled commitment, each transparent admission of a challenge, they were building a different kind of competitive advantage than had existed before.

As more clients began to notice the change, Ethan realized that Brightpath wasn't just recovering from its crisis—it was emerging as a different kind of company altogether.

RECRUITING FOR THE NEW CULTURE

Accountability, Trust

The search for a new CMO seemed like it could take months. Ethan and the executive team had stringent requirements. They needed someone who had the skills and experience to drive Brightpath's marketing efforts but who also aligned with the company's culture and values. Moreover, they needed that person in a hurry.

With the experience of Greg's tenure fresh in his mind, Ethan was determined to approach the hiring process differently than he would have in the past. The new CMO would need to be more than just a strong performer—they would need to be a leader who understood the importance of building trust, fostering collaboration, and creating a sustainable work environment.

One evening, as Ethan reviewed another round of résumés, he couldn't shake the feeling that this decision would define the next chapter of Brightpath's journey. The wrong choice could set them back and undo all the progress they had made. But the right choice could propel them forward, solidifying the foundation of trust and accountability that had become the company's hallmark. The next day, he received a call from an industry colleague, someone who had heard about Brightpath's search for a new marketing leader.

"I think I've found someone who could be a great fit for your CMO role, a woman named Sarah," the colleague said. "She's sharp, experienced, and she gets it. She understands that leadership is about more than just results—it's about building a culture."

Ethan was intrigued. "Send me her information. I'd love to meet her."

The colleague agreed, and within minutes, Ethan had the résumé in his inbox. As he scanned the details, something clicked. Sarah had an impressive background in marketing and sales, but what stood out most was her experience in leading teams through major transitions—guiding companies through periods of change while keeping the culture intact.

They ended up interviewing four candidates. To gain a well-rounded perspective on each one, Ethan pulled together an interview panel composed of leaders from different departments. This approach allowed for diverse insights and helped build trust within the team, showing that everyone's perspective mattered in the decision-making process. Before the interview, Ethan briefed the panel on their specific focus areas, ensuring that each member evaluated a different set of capabilities. He asked Emma, for instance, to assess the candidate's approach to team dynamics, while Leah focused on the candidate's experience with strategic planning and business growth. He had people from the marketing team ask specifics about each candidate's functional skills, including the use of channels, the company's online user experience, and data-driven segmentation.

Ethan himself would cover cultural fit, specifically, the candidate's alignment with Brightpath's core values of trust, collaboration, and sustainable growth. In addition to questions about results, Ethan asked questions that revealed how the candidates viewed leadership—how they balanced performance with team well-being, how they inspired loyalty without pushing people to burnout, and how they saw their role as culture-builders. He was looking for someone who could lead with both vision and empathy, creating a foundation for long-term success.

All the interviews with Sarah took place on the same day, all in the same conference room, but at separate times. Ethan's was the last. From the moment they began talking, he could tell that she understood Brightpath's new culture. Her career trajectory was fascinating: she'd started in product marketing at Adobe, then moved to Salesforce during its rapid growth phase, where she'd led their transition to account-based marketing. Most recently, she'd served as VP of marketing at Zendesk, where she'd helped rebuild their market presence after a difficult period.

When Ethan entered the interview room, Sarah carried herself with quiet confidence. After initial pleasantries, Ethan dove straight in.

"What interests you about Brightpath?" he asked.

Sarah's response was immediate and thoughtful. "Companies in transition fascinate me. At Zendesk, we had to rebuild trust with enterprise customers while maintaining our core identity. It's not just about marketing messages—it's about aligning what you say with what you actually do."

"Tell me about that transition at Zendesk."

"We had a trust gap with larger customers. They loved our product but weren't sure we could support enterprise-scale operations. Instead of just telling them we could, we created complete transparency around our infrastructure investments. We invited CTOs to see our operations firsthand. Within eighteen months, enterprise revenue grew 140 percent."

Ethan leaned forward. "And the team dynamics during that growth?"

"That's where a lot of companies stumble," Sarah said, her expression serious. "They push for growth at any cost. At Zendesk, we took a different approach. We mapped out sustainable growth targets and built in recovery time after major campaigns. When someone worked a weekend for a product launch, they got to take those days off the following week. It wasn't just nice to do—it gave us better results. Fresh teams are creative teams."

"What's your take on digital versus traditional channels?"

Sarah smiled. "It's not either-or anymore. At Adobe, I learned that different segments need different approaches. But here's what's interesting—we found that B2B buyers were spending 70 percent of their journey on digital channels but making final decisions based on personal interactions. So we built what we called 'digital-first, human-close' campaigns. They used automation to nurture leads but invested heavily in customer advocacy and peer networking for late-stage conversion."

"And the results?"

"Sales cycles shortened by 40 percent, and customer acquisition costs dropped by 35 percent. But more importantly, the customers we acquired had higher lifetime value because they came in through trust-based relationships."

Ethan shifted gears. "Tell me about a failure."

Sarah didn't hesitate. "At Salesforce, I pushed too hard for an account-based marketing rollout. We had the whole strategy mapped out, but I didn't spend enough time getting buy-in from sales leaders. The program technically worked, but adoption was low. I had to step back, rebuild those relationships, and relaunch with sales as true partners. It taught me that even the best strategy fails without strong relationships."

"How did you rebuild those relationships?"

"One coffee at a time," Sarah said with a slight laugh. "I spent six weeks just listening to sales leaders' concerns. Turned out they had great insights we hadn't considered. We adjusted the program based on their input, and when we relaunched, they were our biggest advocates. The program ended up exceeding targets by 60 percent."

Ethan nodded, appreciating her candor. "What's your framework for building high-performing teams?"

"Trust, autonomy, and purpose," Sarah replied. "At Zendesk, I inherited a demoralized team. Talent was leaving. Creativity was low. The first step was radical transparency—I shared everything, including our challenges and my own uncertainties. Then we rebuilt around clear ownership areas. Instead of micromanaging campaigns, we created mini-CEOs for each market segment. Finally, we connected every initiative to customer impact. Within three quarters, we had the highest employee engagement scores in the company."

The conversation continued, touching on everything from marketing technology to team development. Throughout, Sarah demonstrated not just marketing expertise but a deep appreciation for trust-based organizations with clear accountability for results.

As they wrapped up, Ethan had one final question. "Why leave Zendesk now? You're having success there."

Sarah grew thoughtful. "Brightpath reminds me of why I love this industry. You're not just fixing processes—you're reimagining how a technology company can operate. The equity grant you just implemented? That's exactly the kind of bold move that builds real culture change. I want to be part of writing that story." Then she smiled at Ethan. "And, of course, it's a CMO role—a big step up for me. But if I didn't like the company so much, I wouldn't be here."

After Sarah left, Ethan sat back in his chair, reflecting on the conversation. Her marketing credentials were impeccable, but it was her approach to leadership that stood out. In a way, she embodied exactly what Brightpath was trying to become.

Feedback was positive from everyone on the interview panel. It only took a few days from the interviews to a unanimous decision, to Sarah's appointment.

THE NEW LEADER ARRIVES

Communication, Trust

Sarah walked into Brightpath on her first day as chief marketing officer, feeling the weight of both expectation and skepticism. Greg's departure had left the marketing department in a fragile state. Some of the team felt relieved, seeing it as the end of a grueling, pressure-driven regime. Others remained uneasy. Despite all the energy and success so far, they weren't sure how long Ethan would last as CEO, and now they had someone coming in from outside.

Ethan had been clear with her during their initial conversations. She wasn't just inheriting a department. She was inheriting a team still recovering from the long shadows Greg had cast.

Ethan met Sarah in his office that morning, his usual calm demeanor in place, but his concern for the team's well-being clear.

"Transition is tricky," he said, leaning back in his chair. "You're stepping into a role that's more than just filling a gap. Some of your team members don't know what it feels like to work in a healthier environment."

Sarah nodded, understanding the gravity of the situation. "I've stepped into roles like this before, where the previous leadership was both admired and feared—and for good reason."

Ethan smiled, though his eyes remained serious. "I trust you. You've got the patience and the experience to rebuild this team. But don't expect an immediate embrace—they're cautious, and some remain loyal to Greg's results-driven approach."

"I'm prepared for that," Sarah said, her voice steady. "Change isn't quick, and it's not always comfortable."

・・・

Sarah spent her first few weeks at Brightpath observing. She resisted the temptation to make sweeping changes, instead focusing on understanding the team dynamics and individual strengths.

She knew the department had limited patience for introductory meetings, but she conducted one anyway during the end of her third week. It was her first major pivotal moment. She was explaining her approach to quarterly targets.

"We're not going to reduce the targets," she said. "But we're going to work smarter to reach them. My goal is to create a sustainable environment—one where you're not burning out by the end of each quarter. That means communicating openly about what's working and what isn't."

A hand shot up from the back of the room—Helen, a relatively junior member of the team, who had been with the company for just under a year. "What happens if we don't meet those targets?" she asked, her voice edged with anxiety. "Under Greg, that wasn't an option. Greg expected us to push through, no matter what."

Sarah paused, letting the room quiet before responding. "Not hitting a target isn't a failure—it's information. It tells us what worked and what didn't. If we don't hit a target, we reassess. We adjust. The goal is to learn and improve, not to punish or push people beyond their limits."

There was a palpable shift in the room. Some team members nodded subtly, while others remained quiet, still processing what Sarah was saying. But for the first time, the seeds of trust were being planted.

Her calendar quickly filled with one-on-one meetings with each member of the department so she could begin to get to know them individually. These meetings provided her with further insight into the team's mindset. It was a department full of talented individuals, many of whom had been pushed to their limits by Greg's leadership.

Meeting with John, one of the senior marketing managers who had been close to Greg, was one of Sarah's more challenging conversations. He sat across from her in the small meeting room, arms folded, his posture radiating defensiveness.

"Greg knew how to push us to get results," John said, his tone clipped. "It wasn't always pleasant, but he got us there. I'm not sure how this new, softer approach is going to work. We're in a competitive market. We don't have the luxury of slowing down."

Sarah listened carefully, her expression open but thoughtful. "I understand your concerns, John. Greg achieved significant results, and I respect that. But I have seen results improve even more when you treat people with respect. And I can show you how to do it."

John's posture remained tense. "I just don't want us to lose our edge."

Sarah leaned forward slightly. "What's more important—hitting a target for one quarter or building a team that can hit those targets quarter after quarter?"

John hesitated, his defensiveness wavering. "I guess we'll see," he mumbled.

Sarah knew that earning John's trust—and the trust of others like him—would take time. But it was a challenge she was ready for.

As the days turned into weeks, Sarah began making changes in the department's structures and practices. For instance, she instituted biweekly team check-ins that encouraged open dialogue. These meetings weren't just about reviewing numbers. They talked through the roadblocks and challenges the team was facing. Greg had insisted that everyone who raised a problem should also suggest a solution. Sarah wanted the teams to think about both the problems and possible solutions together.

Working with Emma's team, she also set up a new system for sharing marketing data—and, more importantly, using that as a starting point for conversation with the other teams. Since they were largely a B2B company, they began looking at their own data related to growth industries. The growth of the chemical industry in India, for instance, brought them a number of new customers whom they would not have approached if it weren't for a joint meeting with the innovation team.

Gradually, Sarah saw small but significant changes in the team's dynamics. The omnipresent tension began to ease. Team members spoke up more during meetings, sharing ideas that they might have previously kept to themselves. Sarah's open-door policy wasn't just a formality—employees were taking her up on it, dropping by to discuss everything from project roadblocks to new ideas.

Ethan noticed the change, too. During one of their weekly check-ins, he asked Sarah how she thought the team was adjusting.

"They're starting to trust me," Sarah said, though her tone was cautious. "There's still some resistance, especially from the people who thrived under Greg's leadership, but we're getting there."

Then, as always, they talked about how to accelerate the process: shorter meetings, more opportunities for people to take charge, better internal user interfaces, and more attention paid to feedback from the teams.

One of the most significant changes Sarah introduced was a fresh approach to performance reviews. Rather than focusing solely on numbers and results, she introduced a more holistic view—one that included feedback on teamwork, communication, and overall well-being. During the first round of these new reviews, Sarah sat down with John once again.

"I've noticed a shift in your work over the past few weeks," she said. "You're still delivering, but I've also seen you step up in helping the newer members of the team. That's the leadership we need—supporting your team members' progress."

John, who had remained somewhat distant in their previous interactions, seemed surprised. "I didn't realize you'd noticed."

"I notice everything," Sarah replied with a smile. "Leadership isn't just about results—it's about how you bring people along with you. And you're doing that."

John nodded slowly, processing her words. "Maybe this approach isn't so bad after all," he said, a small smile creeping onto his face.

• • •

By the end of Sarah's first quarter at Brightpath, the marketing department had transformed. While there was still work to be done, the team had begun to shift from a culture of fear and pressure to one of collaboration and mutual support. Performance was growing steadily, which was much more sustainable than bursts of achievement followed by burnout.

Ethan, who had been monitoring Sarah's progress closely, went to her office at the end of the quarter. As they sat down to review the department's performance, he smiled.

"You've done well, Sarah," he said. "I can see the improvement in the numbers and in the way the team interacts. Honestly, I used to be afraid to come to this floor. Now, I feel welcome here, and I think everyone else does, too."

Her positive review gave Sarah a sense of accomplishment, but also a renewed sense of responsibility. She agreed that she had earned the team's trust for now—no small feat in itself. However, maintaining it would be an ongoing process. It would require constant attention, clear communication, and a commitment to balancing performance with well-being.

After walking with Ethan to the elevator, she passed by the marketing team's conference room. John was leading a small group discussion, his previously skeptical attitude replaced with quiet confidence. Helen was working on a new campaign, her energy far more positive than when Sarah had first met her.

Sarah smiled to herself. Change was happening—slowly but surely. And this was only the beginning.

PROJECT ALIGN

Communication and Accountability

As Brightpath settled into a steady growth rhythm, Ethan knew that the next phase of the company's evolution would involve deeper work on communication and accountability—not just as ideals, but as practices embedded in the company's fabric.

Greg's closed mindset had taught them all a valuable lesson: results without accountability could lead to short-term wins but long-term instability. Ethan wanted to ensure that every department, every team, and every individual understood that success wasn't just a matter of hitting targets. How they hit those targets and how they communicated transparently were critically important skills. Everyone would have to learn them; in fact, they'd have to practice them until they became second nature and adopted as their new normal.

Halfway through his first year as CEO, Ethan gathered the executive team to discuss the next big initiative for Brightpath. The team was a cohesive unit by now; around the table and on screen, they all leaned in to listen to one another. Ethan leaned forward, too, his expression serious but calm.

"We need to focus more on two critical elements," he began. "Transparent communication and accountability. It's not enough to be trustworthy. We need to be clear about expectations, and we need to hold one another accountable to meet those expectations."

Sarah, having already implemented a system of open feedback and communication within her department, spoke up. "In marketing, we've started using open feedback loops that have really transformed how the team operates. People feel more comfortable speaking up when something isn't working, and that transparency has allowed us to address issues before they become major problems."

"What are open feedback loops?" asked Rajiv, the CFO.

"They're biweekly sessions," said Sarah. "Their purpose is to raise problems and close the gap between the current way and the way we'd like it to be." She went on to describe how she set an informal tone at the sessions, encouraging employees to voice their concerns and ideas in an open, supportive environment, while also discussing team performance and the well-being of individual members. "The loop part is that at the end, someone offers to take on each of the challenges we've found. They iterate a fix of some sort, and then at a later date, we get further feedback on how the fix turned out."

She shared some of the remarks that people had made about the feedback sessions. John, the senior marketing manager who had been skeptical of Sarah's leadership style, had admitted: "This new system has been a game-changer for me. At first, I thought it was just going to slow us down, but being able to bring up issues and get feedback in real time has actually made us more efficient."

Helen, the recent recruit who had worried about pressure, had said: "I feel like I can actually ask for help now without feeling like I'm going to be judged. Before, it was like if you couldn't keep up, you just had to figure it out on your own. Now, it feels more like I'm part of a team."

"The feedback loop sessions had become spaces," Sarah said, "where the teams felt heard, valued, and supported." And the results were impressive. Productivity was up and, in a recent employee survey, morale was higher than it had been in years.

Leah, the VP of operations, nodded in agreement. "Operations could definitely benefit from that kind of approach. Right now, we have performance reviews, but they're very top-down. There's not a lot of opportunity for teams to give feedback to their managers, and I think that's holding us back."

Ethan saw the momentum building. "I like this. What Sarah's done in marketing is a model for the entire company. We need to create systems that encourage open, two-way communication. And that communication needs to lead to real accountability—on both sides."

Rajiv, the CFO, chimed in. "How do you see accountability working beyond just performance metrics? We've always tracked results, but I know you're talking about something more than that."

Ethan leaned back in his chair, considering the question. "Accountability isn't just about whether we hit our numbers—it's about how we get there. Are we communicating openly about challenges? Are we supporting each other when roadblocks come up? And most importantly, are we visibly taking responsibility for maintaining the culture we've built?"

• • •

Thus, *Project Align* was born. The initiative focused on fostering transparent communication and mutual accountability across the entire company. Ethan clarified that this wasn't just another corporate program—it was the next step in Brightpath's evolution. Ethan tasked every department head with implementing open communication forums where employees could give feedback, ask questions, and discuss goals without fear of repercussions.

Sarah's marketing team's feedback sessions became the model for this initiative. Ethan worked closely with each executive to tailor the approach to their department's needs. In operations, Leah introduced weekly huddles where teams could improve the workflow, identify challenges, and ask for resources. Emma's product team adopted a similar system, integrating feedback processes into their agile sprints to give engineers and designers more voice in the decision-making process.

Meanwhile, Ethan introduced a new company-wide digital app called *The Accountability Matrix*. This tool wasn't just another performance tracker—it was a living document that outlined clear deliverables for each team member, linked to broader company objectives. The most important innovation came from how the team used the matrix. It wasn't just about tracking what employees accomplished. It was about fostering accountability on both sides of the equation.

"*The Accountability Matrix* is designed to be a two-way channel," Ethan explained during a company-wide meeting. "Managers will provide the resources, support, and clear communication their teams need to succeed. Team members can request specific types of support. When we're clear with each other, we can hold each other accountable in a way that's productive, not punitive."

The matrix included sections where employees could give feedback on their manager's communication, support, and leadership. It encouraged a culture of mutual accountability, where leaders were just as responsible for fostering a healthy work environment as their teams were for meeting performance goals.

Project Align

As *The Accountability Matrix* rolled out, Ethan made it a point to check in with different departments to see how it was being received. In a meeting with Leah's operations team, he asked for honest feedback on the new system.

"I'll be honest," said Martin, one of the operations managers. "At first, I thought this was just another way to keep tabs on us. But after using it for a few weeks, I've realized it actually gives me more control over my work. I know exactly what's expected of me, and I can give feedback when things aren't clear. It's made communication with my team a lot smoother."

Leah nodded in agreement. "Transparency is helping us avoid miscommunication, and we're catching issues early. It's also allowed my team to feel more empowered—they're speaking up when they need something, and that's made a big difference in our efficiency."

As the weeks passed, *The Accountability Matrix* became a key tool in Brightpath's operations. Teams across the company saw the benefits of open communication and mutual accountability. Issues that had once caused frustration and delays were now being addressed quickly and efficiently. Managers were more in tune with their teams, and employees felt more supported and empowered. The client-facing teams also began using it to jointly manage projects, with Metro Industries leading the way.

With these two methodologies in place, improvement became more visible. Brightpath was becoming a healthier, more transparent, more productive organization. Communication flowed more freely, people embraced rather than feared accountability, and the company's culture of trust grew into its greatest asset.

Around this time, the trial of Victor and Jennifer began. While the press covered them extensively, none of their transgressions tainted

Brightpath. Instead, business reporters typically mentioned Brightpath as the firm that had thrown out its founder, instituted employee stock ownership, and won back its reputation. When Victor and Jennifer were ultimately convicted of fraud and stock manipulation in a jury trial, Tanya and Ethan were featured in articles about their alternative path to growth.

We're finally hitting our stride, Ethan thought one afternoon as he walked through the office, watching the teams collaborate with a sense of purpose and camaraderie. It was the company he had always wanted to be a part of, where trust, communication, and accountability weren't just buzzwords, but the foundation of everything they did. *And this is just the beginning*, he said to himself.

THE FOUR-FIFTY CRISIS

Trust, Accountability, and Communication

The first signs of trouble appeared quietly, almost like a whisper in the wind. One of Brightpath's key American clients, Meridian Healthcare, emailed with a subtle but pointed question: "How is Brightpath planning to keep pace with Four-Fifty?"

The company Four-Fifty had seemed like a minor threat when Obie first flagged them six months ago. Started just two years earlier by three AI researchers—from Estonia, Finland, and Moldova, respectively—they'd relocated to Austin's tech corridor with seed funding from Andreessen Horowitz.

Ethan forwarded the email to Emma immediately. Within minutes, his screen lit up with a video call request.

"I think we have a problem," Emma said without preamble, her London office visible behind her. "Four-Fifty just released their integration suite. It's... well, you need to see this." She shared her screen, showing a demo video.

"Talk to me about what I'm seeing," Ethan said, watching as the system seamlessly connected with various enterprise platforms.

"They've built something we discussed two years ago but deemed too resource-intensive," Emma said, frustration evident in her voice. "They're using large language models to create natural interfaces between different enterprise systems. No coding required. Their system learns each platform's architecture and creates bridges automatically."

"And it works?"

"Better than it should, since the company is just starting out," Emma admitted. "They've leveraged some of the new GenAI tools in ways we haven't considered. While we were focused on stabilizing our core platform after the crisis, they fundamentally reimagined the integration problem and developed an impressive solution."

Ethan leaned back in his chair. "You've been tracking them. Why didn't we see this coming?"

Emma was quiet for a moment. "Honestly? We got comfortable. Their early products were basic—faster and cheaper, yes, but limited. We assumed they'd stay in that lane." She paused. "But there's more. They're not just using AI for integration. They've built what they call 'predictive workflow optimization.' Their system doesn't just connect platforms; it learns how organizations use them and suggests process improvements."

"Like our analytics suite?"

"More advanced. Our system provides insights. Theirs actually implements changes in real time, with user permission. And because it's built on these new language models, it can explain its recommendations in natural language that makes sense to business users."

Ethan felt a knot forming in his stomach. "Cost comparison?"

"Their full enterprise suite is priced at 40 percent below our base platform. And they're offering free migrations." Emma ran a hand through her hair, a rare sign of stress from the usually composed

CTO. "We're not just losing the price war anymore, Ethan. They've leapfrogged us technologically."

By Wednesday morning, the situation had escalated. Meridian Healthcare wasn't the only one asking questions. Three other major clients had reached out, all mentioning Four-Fifty's new capabilities. The startup had orchestrated a perfect storm: a splashy product launch backed by impressive technical innovations and aggressive pricing.

Ethan called an emergency executive team meeting. As Sarah, Leah, Rajiv, and Emma joined—some in person, others virtually—he could see the concern on their faces. They'd all been so focused on rebuilding trust, improving processes, and stabilizing the company that they'd missed a tectonic shift in their market.

"Before we start," Ethan said, "I want to acknowledge something. We've done incredible work rebuilding Brightpath's foundation. But while we were looking inward, the market changed. Now we have to prove we can innovate while maintaining the trust we've rebuilt."

Leah was the first to speak. "I've already heard from several key accounts—they're concerned that we're not innovating quickly enough. Some are even threatening to pull their contracts if we can't convince them we're still the better choice."

Emma spoke up from the video screen. "I've been running analyses since Monday. Four-Fifty isn't just a competitor with a good product. They represent a fundamental shift in how enterprise software operates. Their system is built for a world where AI doesn't just assist—it actively participates in business."

"Can we catch up?" Sarah asked, voicing what everyone was thinking.

"That's the wrong question," Emma replied. "We need to leap ahead of them. I have some ideas, but they're not incremental improvements. We'd need to rethink our entire approach to AI integration."

Ethan looked around the room, seeing both concern and determination on his team members' faces. They had rebuilt Brightpath's culture around trust and accountability. Now they would have to prove that this foundation could support rapid innovation without sacrificing their values.

"Okay," he said. "Emma, you have the floor. Show us the future."

"We've been working on our next-generation version," Emma said, "but it's not ready for launch. We can speed up development, but we can't rush it. If we push too fast, we risk releasing something subpar, and that will only make things worse."

Ethan nodded, understanding the fine line they were walking. "I agree. Rushing the product to market isn't the answer. We need to maintain our reputation for quality, but we also can't ignore the fact that clients are looking for faster, more affordable solutions."

Sarah, who had been carefully considering her next words, finally spoke. "We need to get ahead of the narrative," she said. "Clients are already questioning our competitiveness, and if we stay silent, we'll lose their trust. We need to be transparent—acknowledge that we're working on something even better, but we can't promise what we can't deliver. We need to communicate what makes our product superior without making empty promises."

Rajiv, ever focused on the financial impact, chimed in. "These clients are too important to lose. If they cancel, it'll affect more than just this quarter—it'll shake the confidence of the board."

"Rather than stay with the next-generation version as is," Emma said, "we need to take it past where Four-Fifty has gone. I think we should start with customer needs. Sarah, you and I have enough data between us to see what's missing from the Four-Fifty platform. If we can focus on those gaps, maybe we can leapfrog them just as they've leapfrogged us."

"That's a start," Ethan said. He stood up, pacing the room as he thought. "This is more than just a product issue. It's a trust issue. Clients need to believe that we're still the best choice, even if we're still in development. We need to reassure them, but we also need to deliver something that justifies their faith in us."

The room was silent for a moment, the weight of the decision pressing down on everyone. Finally, Ethan spoke again, his voice resolute. "We will not panic. We're going to be strategic. Emma, please speed up this new product development angle. Consider every alternative except one: don't compromise quality. Sarah, I want you to take the lead on client communication. It's not just about surveying them. We need to send out a clear, honest message that reassures our clients and highlights what sets us apart."

Sarah nodded. "I'll craft the messaging, but we'll need to be consistent across the board—no mixed signals. If we start over-promising, it'll backfire."

Ethan agreed. "We'll be transparent. Clients need to know that we're working on something better, but we won't make promises we can't keep. Leah, please work with the operations team to ensure flawless delivery of our current orders. If we can't innovate as fast as the competition, we need to at least maintain our reputation for reliability."

They set the plan and dispersed, each leader knowing the gravity of the task ahead.

• • •

The next few weeks were some of the most intense in Brightpath's recent history. Emma's product team worked around the clock, balancing three daunting pressures at once: to speed up development, to maintain their standards for quality, and to leapfrog to the next generation of products and services. Emma held daily check-ins with her engineers, ensuring that they had the resources they needed, while also keeping a close eye on timelines.

"We're taking risks in our concept," she reminded her team during one meeting, "but we can't afford mistakes in execution. This product needs to be flawless, or we'll lose more than just contracts—we'll lose our reputation."

Meanwhile, Sarah's marketing teams were in full crisis-management mode. She gathered her team in the marketing department's war room, the walls lined with client reports, competitive analysis, and draft messaging.

"This is about trust," Sarah said, addressing the team. "Our clients are nervous, and we need to reassure them we're not just keeping up—we're surpassing the competition. But we can't lie to them. Our message needs to be honest, clear, and consistent."

Her team got to work crafting emails, press releases, and making client calls that struck the delicate balance between reassurance and transparency. Sarah now handled the most important accounts, making sure they understood Brightpath was still their best option, even if the competitor had gotten to the market first.

Ethan monitored the situation closely, holding daily check-ins with each department to ensure alignment. He was careful to stay visible—walking through the office, stopping by different departments, and holding impromptu meetings to address concerns. The crisis had rattled the company, but Ethan knew that his calm and confident leadership would be the key to keeping everyone focused.

⋯

A month into the crisis, Brightpath was stabilizing. Emma and Sarah had indeed collaborated on client research, and they'd come up with a way to define the new offering.

"Look, Four-Fifty's platform is impressive," Emma told the group, "but it's still fundamentally reactive. It waits for systems to connect, then builds bridges. What I'm proposing is predictive integration. Our system would anticipate a company's ambitions and help them build the capabilities they need in advance. For example, if they're considering a major move—like launching a product line or addressing a competitive threat—our system will be like a GPS for strategic execution. It will offer our clients a step-by-step map to reach their next business goals and help them build and adapt the capabilities they'll need to overcome the challenges along the way. For instance, if they would benefit from entering a new geographic market, even if they haven't considered it yet, our new software can automatically prepare the necessary system connections, data frameworks, and compliance protocols."

"And we can then track what happens next," Rajiv added, "and keep improving our predictions."

"Yes," said Emma. "While Four-Fifty focuses on connecting existing systems, we'll provide system evolution."

"Four-Fifty will be doing much the same," Ethan objected. "So will all the other companies, including the likes of Salesforce and Oracle. If we get an edge there, it won't last long."

"That's why trust matters," Sarah replied, jumping in. "Our clients all know that the technology is like a commodity. Our differentiator is our cultural values—trust, accountability, and communication. They know we'll tell them the truth about what we're doing, that we'll keep our promises, and that we'll pay close attention to what they tell us."

She went on to say something that none of them had ever quite thought of this way before. "Our clients also know that if anyone in our company loses their way, even the CEO, CFO, or CMO, we'll hold them accountable. The rest of us will stay afloat. They know it, because we've already done it."

None of the other executive team members had that perspective, Ethan thought. It took someone who was outside the company when all those things happened.

While Four-Fifty's product continued to make waves in the market, Brightpath held onto most of its key clients. Thanks to the clear and consistent communication Sarah's team had orchestrated. But the next challenge was still ahead—Brightpath's new product had to deliver.

At the two-month mark, Ethan gathered the executive team for an update on the product's progress. Emma, looking tired but determined, was the first to speak. "We're on track for a release in six more weeks. The engineering team has been working day and night, and I'm confident this product will not only match the competition, but it will also exceed our clients' expectations."

Sarah added, "We've kept the messaging consistent—clients know we're taking our time to ensure quality. But we need to be prepared for the launch. This product has to be error-free, and we need to be ready with a strong marketing push to go alongside it."

Leah nodded. "The operations team is ready to scale once the product is completed. We've prepped our teams for the rollout, and we've smoothed out any potential bottlenecks in production."

Rajiv, ever the realist, pointed out the financial stakes. "If this product doesn't land, we're going to be in trouble. We've already taken a hit this quarter, and investors are watching closely."

Ethan took a deep breath. "I know. But we will not rush this. The product will be ready when it's ready, and when it launches, it will show our clients why they've stayed with us. We've been through crises before, and we've come out stronger. This will be no different."

• • •

As the launch date approached, tension throughout Brightpath reached new heights. Emma's team pushed to meet deadlines, while Sarah's marketing teams prepared for the rollout. Ethan made it a point to stay present, walking through departments and checking in with teams, both in the office and remote, to make sure everyone felt supported.

People worked long hours, but the expectations were different this time. The company took care to make sure everyone had at least one day off per week. If there were unforeseen challenges threatening a milestone, management was accountable for moving around resources. Ethan and the other executive team leaders took the opportunity to streamline the workflow further. It was interesting how much red tape could be cut when people trusted one another. The company's reputation and culture also made it easier to find a few subcontractors they trusted who could be called in to handle discrete projects. The team reorganization also bore fruit in this cycle; it gave everyone a primary priority to focus on, while keeping them available for internal advice and consultation.

On the day of the product's launch, Ethan called a town hall meeting. The launch was a resounding success, and Ethan couldn't help but feel a swell of pride as he walked into the packed conference room. A standing ovation greeted the project team, whose innovative new software had not only met but exceeded expectations—and sparked a wide round of acclaim in the business press.

Leah, the VP of operations, stood at the podium, addressing the room. "I want to recognize the entire team for their incredible work. This wasn't just about hitting deadlines—it was about collaboration, trust, and bringing out the best in each other. This is what Brightpath can achieve when we work as one."

Ethan smiled, watching the team members—some in the room, others joining virtually—exchange high-fives and congratulations. He approached the front of the room as the applause subsided, taking the microphone.

"First off, I want to echo Leah's sentiments," Ethan began. "This success belongs to every single one of you. It's a testament to what happens when we lead with trust, accountability, and a shared purpose."

He glanced at the screens showing the remote participants. "This wasn't just a project—it was a demonstration of what makes Brightpath unique. We've built a culture where every voice matters, where collaboration isn't bound by location, and where everyone—whether in this room or halfway across the world—feels like they're part of something bigger."

Ethan paused, scanning the room. "Some might say it's faster or easier to work the way we used to—top-down, results-driven at all costs. But I'd argue that the way we've approached this project proves something important: trust isn't just a nice-to-have; it's a competitive advantage."

He turned toward Rajiv, the CFO, who nodded in agreement. "The numbers are impressive. Early client feedback shows we're not just meeting expectations—we're setting a new standard. And that's because this team was not just motivated by results; they were also driven to work hard for each other."

As Ethan stepped aside, Leah returned to the podium, smiling. "I think I speak for all of us when I say we're ready for the next challenge."

The room was filled with applause, and Ethan felt a rush of accomplishment. The crisis had tested their resolve, but it had also strengthened the company's foundation. They had faced the storm, and now they were ready to come out stronger on the other side.

BUILDING A NEXT-GENERATION COMPANY

The launch of Brightpath's new platform was a resounding success. The weeks of intense work had paid off, and the company had weathered the storm of competition with its reputation not only intact but strengthened. Clients who had once questioned Brightpath's ability to innovate were now reaffirming their commitment to the company. The crisis that had once threatened to derail everything had been overcome.

Ethan sat in his office late one evening, the lights of the city twinkling through the windows. The office was quiet now, the energy from the launch having given way to a calm, almost serene atmosphere. It was a rare moment of peace, and Ethan took it as an opportunity to reflect on the journey that had brought him and the company to this point.

• • •

There was a knock on the door, and Tanya entered. She moved over to the chair across from Ethan and just sat there, not saying anything.

Ethan let her sit for a moment before he said, "To what do I owe the pleasure?"

"Congratulations," she said. She placed an expensive bottle of champagne on his desk. "Not for now," she said. "This is for you and your wife."

"I appreciate it," he said. "And are we going to look at the future now?"

"We will," she said. "I'll be calling on you. In many ways. But for today, let's just take in the moment."

They sat together, silently, before she excused herself. Ethan remained seated, reflecting on everything Brightpath had been through in the past year. The original crisis, Greg's departure, the Four-Fifty challenge—and, he had to admit, the shift to a new leadership style—had tested him in ways he hadn't expected. Leadership, he realized, wasn't about having all the answers—it was about building the right foundation of trust, communication, and accountability and letting those principles guide the team through uncertainty.

Ethan now understood that leading in the digital age came with unique challenges. But the principles that governed leadership in an office-based team—trust, transparency, and open communication—were even more critical in a dispersed, global workforce.

Sarah's leadership in the marketing department was a testament to that. She had taken a team that had been on the verge of burnout and rebuilt it into a cohesive, collaborative unit that thrived on open communication and mutual respect. Her approach to leadership, which emphasized sustainable success over short-term gains, had become a model for the rest of the company.

The marketing team was now one of the most innovative and collaborative departments in the company. They didn't just hit their targets—they exceeded them, all while maintaining a culture of balance and support. Sarah's leadership had shown that you didn't need to sacrifice well-being for performance. The two could coexist, and in fact, they could enhance one another.

The other departments had also broken through their old patterns. Leah's operations team was now like a well-oiled machine—but not mechanical at all. It had developed its own organic approach, partnering people and tech systems to ensure smooth, efficient production. Rajiv's finance team had taken a more strategic role, helping to align financial goals with the company's broader mission. And Emma's product team had become the heartbeat of Brightpath's innovation engine, consistently pushing the boundaries of what was possible, while maintaining the company's commitment to quality.

Ethan was most proud of the culture they had built. Brightpath transformed from a company prioritizing performance above all else to a company where performance and culture were equally important. Trust, communication, and accountability weren't just words—they were the lifeblood of the organization.

As he considered the road ahead, Ethan knew cultural values were the only way to ensure Brightpath's long-term success. As the company grew, those same values would continue to be the cornerstone of everything they did.

• • •

Ethan stood up from his desk and walked to the large windows that overlooked the city. The lessons learned over the past year would serve them well as they moved forward. The crisis to beat their new competitor had shown them that the market was constantly changing, and Brightpath couldn't afford to rest on its laurels.

He thought about the team—the executive team, the engineers, the marketers, the operations staff, and the remote employees scattered across different time zones. They were the ones who had built Brightpath into what it was today, and they were the ones who would take it into the future.

The following morning, Ethan convened a town hall meeting for the entire company, both in-office and remote. The energy in the room was different now, more confident, more unified. Although the launch succeeded, the team was clearly already focused on what would come next.

As Ethan stood before them, he smiled. "We've been through a lot this year," he began, his voice carrying through the room. "There were moments when it felt like everything was on the line. But each time, we pulled together. We communicated, we trusted each other, and we held ourselves accountable. And because of that, we didn't just survive—we thrived."

The room was quiet, but there was a palpable sense of pride and accomplishment in the air.

"We've built something special with this company," Ethan continued. "It's not just about the products we make or the clients we serve—it's about the culture we've created. It's not even about the paychecks or the equity we share. It is the culture of trust, transparency, and accountability that sets us apart. And that's what's going to carry us forward."

He paused, letting the words sink in.

"But this isn't the end of the journey," he said, his tone shifting to one of anticipation. "The market is always changing, and we need to keep evolving. We need to stay innovative, stay focused, and, most importantly, stay true to who we are. The challenges will keep coming, but I know that we're ready to face them—together."

The room erupted into applause, and Ethan felt a surge of energy. This was what leadership was about—not just guiding a company through tough times, but building something that could stand the test of time.

. . .

As the meeting ended and the team dispersed, Ethan stayed behind for a moment, watching as people chatted, laughed, and moved on to their next tasks. He could see the confidence in their faces, the sense of ownership they felt over their work, and the company's success. Brightpath was ready for whatever came next. And Ethan knew, more than ever, that the company's future was bright—not just because of the products they would create, but because of the people who would create them.

PART TWO

LEADERSHIP THEORY AND PRACTICAL APPLICATION

INTRODUCING PART TWO

Leading a hybrid organization like Brightpath is a challenge that demands more than just strategy—it requires vision, adaptability, and the courage to lead through complexity. Ethan's story illuminates the transformative power of trust, accountability, and transparent communication in uniting a global team across diverse locations and time zones. It's a journey that reveals what true leadership looks like in the digital age.

As we move on to Part Two, it's important to recognize how the core pillars of leadership that have been discussed—**Trust**, **Communication**, and **Accountability**—shape a successful and cohesive team. These three components form the foundation of effective leadership and create a resilient, high-performing team culture. Each is powerful on its own, but their potential is truly unlocked when they're used in concert, each one reinforcing and strengthening the others. As illustrated in the following diagram, imagine them as a cycle, connected by arrows, with each component driving and depending on the others to achieve sustainable results.

THE CORE PILLARS OF LEADERSHIP

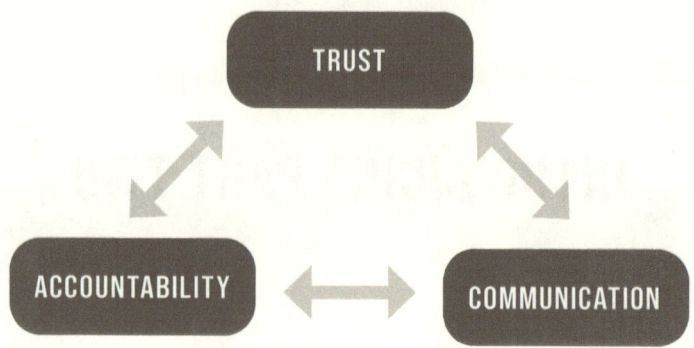

The first and most important pillar is **Trust**. When team members trust one another, they feel safe sharing ideas, voicing concerns, and taking risks. Without trust, teams struggle to collaborate effectively, as individuals hold back, fearing judgment or repercussions. Leaders must actively cultivate trust by demonstrating consistency, transparency, and a commitment to the team's well-being.

Communication serves as the essential bridge that connects trust to accountability. Open and transparent communication channels enable team members to stay informed, share feedback, and remain aligned on goals and expectations. Communication isn't simply about passing along information; it's about creating a space for dialogue, listening actively, and fostering understanding. Leaders who communicate openly build credibility and capability. They inspire a dynamic flow of ideas and insights. They create teams that are more powerful working together than they are as individuals.

Accountability binds the core pillars together, setting clear standards and holding each person responsible for their role in the team's success. Accountability strengthens trust by ensuring that each individual follows through on commitments and aligns with shared values.

When accountability is present, trust deepens, and communication flourishes, as team members know they can rely on one another to deliver results.

Together, trust, communication, and accountability create a powerful, mutually reinforcing cycle that supports every interaction and decision within a team. In the chapters that follow, we will explore practical strategies for building each element in your leadership practice. By embracing this interconnected model, leaders can create an environment where each team member feels valued, supported, and empowered to contribute to the organization's shared vision.

Why does this model work, especially in today's complex and fast-paced work environments? At its core, this approach embraces a simple yet transformative truth: organizations are primarily groups of people, and people excel when they feel valued, empowered, and aligned with a shared purpose.

Now, let's dive deeper into exploring how these concepts can apply to your own leadership journey. Each chapter in Part Two will unpack a specific leadership lesson. They will draw on the story of Ethan and Brightpath, offering practical tools, strategies, and insights to help you lead more effectively, whether your team is across the hall or across the world.

BUILDING TRUST AS THE FOUNDATION OF LEADERSHIP

People frequently discuss trust, and while nearly everyone thinks they understand the term, they often misunderstand it. Trust is the mutual belief in the reliability, integrity, and intentions of others. The others could be members of your team, your organization, your customer or client base, your value chain, or your society. Trust—or the lack of it—shapes the quality and outcome of every human interaction.

In leadership, a high level of trust means that team members believe in their leader's ability to make sound decisions, their honesty and transparency, and their commitment to the team's well-being and success. It also means that leaders trust their team to perform their duties with competence and adherence to shared values.

Trust is the bedrock of any successful team, organization, or relationship. Without it, even the most talented individuals cannot work together, and the most innovative strategies can collapse under the weight of suspicion or uncertainty. As a leader, building and maintaining trust is not just an ideal—it is essential.

How do you build that trust? And, once you've built it, how do you ensure it endures through challenges and crises?

The answer lies in consistent, authentic leadership practices.

THE ROLE OF TRUST IN LEADERSHIP

Trust is often seen as intangible—a soft skill that's difficult to measure but vital to success. In reality, trust is tangible through action. It manifests in many small ways: in how your team communicates, how you all handle challenges, and how willing you all are to take risks and innovate.

Think back to Ethan's journey at Brightpath. Early on, when he took over as CEO, he inherited a culture where trust was largely absent. Major structural forces, symbolized by the duplicity of Victor and Jennifer, the old CEO and CFO, made it almost impossible to trust one another. While most organizations don't have that kind of explicit trust crisis at the top, many do have scandals come to light. Recent examples include companies like Boeing, Meta, OpenAI, and Wells Fargo. Even relatively stable organizations generally keep the reasons for their strategic decisions hidden. This may give them a competitive advantage, but lack of transparency also erodes trust. Trust is impacted when people can't understand why the company is making its decisions.

Under Greg's leadership, trust eroded through several common problems, all wrapped up in his top-down management style. Greg's intense focus on results disregarded the value of people's efforts and open communication. His tendency to micromanage left team members feeling stifled and undervalued. His teams were hesitant to take the initiative or share new ideas. Greg's lack of transparency around decisions led to uncertainty and rumors, creating a disconnect between him and the team. His emphasis on individual achievements over collective success fostered competition instead of collaboration, thereby weakening team cohesion. This environment ultimately left employees feeling disconnected and disengaged, highlighting the urgent need to rebuild trust as a foundation for strong, cohesive leadership.

Despite Greg's convincing performance reflected in the numbers, his toxic behavior had created an atmosphere of fear and pressure. Team members didn't feel safe voicing concerns or offering new ideas. They conducted their work in isolation, constantly worried about meeting Greg's often unrealistic expectations.

Ethan recognized that building trust had to come before optimizing performance. He knew that if they didn't take time to build trust among employees and leaders, the company would continue to struggle—no matter how talented the team was. His decision to part ways with Greg was based on this insight. He only made that decision after Greg refused to change his attitude. Ethan couldn't keep him on the team because Brightpath desperately needed to build a culture where people felt safe, supported, and able to collaborate without fear. Otherwise, it could not compete in the new competitive digital marketplace.

HOW TO BUILD TRUST AS A LEADER

Building trust isn't something that happens overnight. Trust is organic and needs time to grow. As noted in this model, which my colleagues and I call The Pyramid of Trust, it requires transparency, consistency, vulnerability, and empathy.

THE PYRAMID OF TRUST

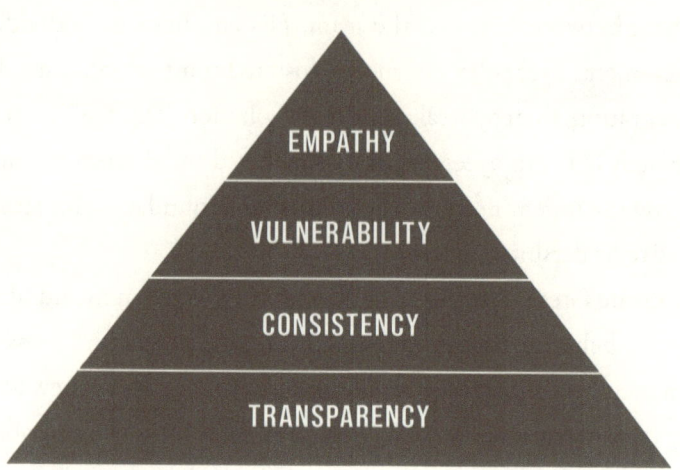

Here are a few key practices that help establish and strengthen trust in any organization:

1. Be Transparent

As a leader, you must be open and honest with your team, even when the news isn't good. Whether it's discussing the company's financial situation, acknowledging mistakes, or addressing difficult feedback, your team needs to know that you're not hiding things from them.

In the story, Ethan demonstrated transparency through his leadership by addressing the team directly during moments of crisis. He revealed sensitive information to the extent he could, including news about Victor, the fact that he personally had fired Greg, and the reasons why he hired Sarah. When competitor Four-Fifty launched its product and clients started questioning Brightpath's ability to compete, Ethan didn't sugarcoat the situation. He didn't promise solutions he couldn't deliver. Instead, he communicated clearly, outlining what the company was working on and why they needed to focus on quality over speed.

> **Practical Tip:** Make a habit of sharing updates with your team, even when the information will be hard for them to hear. By being open, you show you trust your team to handle the truth—and that builds reciprocal trust.

2. Be Consistent

Consistent actions, not just words, build trust over time. If you say you're going to do something, follow through. If you establish expectations, hold yourself and your team accountable to them. Consistency shows that you are reliable, and your team will know they can count on you.

Ethan didn't just talk about changing Brightpath's culture—he made consistent, deliberate efforts to do so. Whether it was by practicing active listening consistently, creating open feedback channels with Sarah, or implementing *The Accountability Matrix*, Ethan took actions that reinforced his commitment to rebuilding trust.

> **Practical Tip:** Be consistent in both your words and actions. Show fairness, respect, and support to everyone, regardless of their role. Trust and morale grow when your team knows they will be treated with consistency and integrity.

3. Demonstrate Vulnerability

Many leaders think they need to have all the answers or never show weakness, but in reality, vulnerability can be a powerful tool for building trust. Admitting when you don't know something or acknowledging mistakes shows you are human. It invites your team to do the same, fostering a culture where people feel safe being open and honest.

In the story, Ethan wasn't afraid to show vulnerability at several points. He let the executive team members and the members of the marketing department know that he needed their skills and participation. He acknowledged the challenges Brightpath was facing and was transparent about the fact that they needed time to respond properly. By being open about the company's position, he gained the team's respect and trust.

> **Practical Tip:** The next time you're unsure of a solution or have made a mistake, don't cover it up. Admit it to your team and invite them to help solve the problem. This will show that you trust them, and in return, they will trust you more.

4. Show Empathy

Trust is rooted in relationships, and relationships are built through empathy. Understanding your team's perspectives, listening to their concerns, and recognizing their contributions helps create a bond of trust. When people feel seen and valued, they are more likely to trust their leader and each other.

Sarah's way of taking over the leadership of the marketing team was an example of empathy in action. She didn't come in and demand immediate changes. Instead, she spent weeks meeting with each team member, understanding their struggles, and slowly building a more supportive and collaborative environment. Her empathy allowed her to earn the team's trust, even in a department that had been wary of change. Ethan also demonstrated empathy when he would openly talk about why people acted the way they did—for example, when he tells Greg he understands his frustration or when he and Tanya consider the motives of the clients who withdrew their businesses.

> **Practical Tip:** Take time to get to know your team. Ask them about their challenges, their goals, and their concerns. Listen actively and show that you value their input. Empathy goes a long way in building trust.

MAINTAINING TRUST THROUGH CHALLENGES

Once established, trust requires equally diligent maintenance, especially during crises or periods of change. Challenges will arise, whether as external market pressures, internal team dynamics, or personal setbacks. How you lead through those moments determines whether trust strengthens or erodes.

During all four crises in the story—the original Victor/Jennifer departure, the quality crisis, the firing of Greg, and the Four-Fifty competition—Brightpath faced significant pressure. Clients questioned the company's ability to innovate, and the team was stretched to its limits. But Ethan maintained the trust he had built by staying calm, communicating openly, and reinforcing the company's values. He didn't make empty promises, and he didn't panic. His steady leadership showed the team that even in difficult times, they could trust him to guide them through the storm.

PRACTICAL APPLICATIONS:
HOW TO BUILD TRUST IN YOUR ORGANIZATION

1. Assess Your Current Level of Trust

Take a step back and evaluate where you stand with your team. Do people feel safe sharing their concerns? Are they comfortable coming to you with feedback? If not, what might hold them back? Use these insights to pinpoint areas needing improved trust.

2. Create Regular Feedback Loops

Establish consistent, open channels for feedback—both from you to your team and from your team to you. Regular check-ins, team meetings, and one-on-one conversations are great ways to ensure that communication stays open and that trust remains a two-way street.

3. Demonstrate Accountability

One of the fastest ways to lose trust is by refusing to take accountability. Hold yourself to the same standards you set for your team. If you make a mistake, own it. If a project doesn't go as planned, lead the way in addressing the problem rather than shifting blame. Ethan made a point of doing this several times while asking executive team members or others to let him know if he overstepped.

4. Build Relationships Beyond Work

People often build trust outside of formal work settings. Take the time to get to know your team on a personal level. Ask about their hobbies, their families, and what drives them. Building those connections fosters a deeper sense of trust and loyalty.

TRUST IS AN ONGOING COMMITMENT

Building trust is not a onetime task—it's an ongoing commitment. Every interaction, every decision, and every communication either strengthens or weakens the trust between you and your team. As a leader, it's your responsibility to prioritize trust every day. By being transparent, consistent, vulnerable, and empathetic, you create an environment where trust can flourish, and with it, the success of your team and organization.

In the next chapter, we will explore how transparent communication builds on this foundation of trust, helping you to further strengthen your leadership and foster collaboration within your team.

TRANSPARENT COMMUNICATION

Once trust is established as the foundation of leadership, we must ensure open and honest communication throughout the organization. Transparent communication is the bridge between trust and accountability—it allows team members to align with organizational goals, address challenges early, and feel valued as contributors.

Transparency isn't just about sharing information. It includes creating an environment where people feel safe expressing their opinions, voicing concerns, and offering ideas. When communication is transparent, it eliminates confusion, reduces misunderstandings, and fosters a culture where trust can flourish.

WHY TRANSPARENT COMMUNICATION MATTERS

Leaders must use clear and open communication to ensure their teams align with the organization's mission, values, and goals. Without transparency, gaps in information can lead to frustration, poor decision-making, and even mistrust. It creates situations where people don't know how their work contributes to a larger whole or which priorities to put first. Often, it's difficult to ask directly, so most employees tend to guess—and that can lead to decisions that may cause problems immediately or in the future. Moreover, leaders who keep information to themselves or cannot communicate clearly risk losing the trust they've worked hard to build.

Take Sarah's leadership in the marketing department at Brightpath. Before Sarah took over, Greg's closed, top-down communication style had become the norm for the team. Team members felt they had little input in decision-making, and this led to resentment and disengagement. Sarah recognized that to rebuild the department, she had to break down those communication barriers. She instituted regular feedback loops in the form of biweekly conversations, encouraging team members to voice their concerns and ideas. This transparency allowed the team to address issues early and work more collaboratively, ultimately improving morale and performance.

TRANSPARENT COMMUNICATION: THE FIVE-STEP MODEL FOR EFFECTIVE LEADERSHIP

Transparent communication is more than sharing information—it's about fostering understanding, alignment, and accountability at every level of an organization. This five-step model breaks down the process into actionable stages that build trust, encourage collaboration, and empower teams.

1. Start with Clear Intentions

Communication begins with clarity. Leaders must clearly articulate their goals and the purpose behind their message. When intentions are clear, it reduces misunderstandings and sets the tone for focused, purposeful dialogue.

2. Explain Why the Issue Is Important

The "why" matters. People are more likely to engage when they understand the significance of the task or decision at hand. By explaining why something is important, leaders connect the immediate conversation to broader goals, fostering a sense of purpose and ownership.

3. Foster Two-Way Communication

Great communication is a dialogue, not a monologue. Leaders must create opportunities for feedback, encouraging employees to share their thoughts, ask questions, and express concerns. Two-way communication builds a culture of respect and collaboration, ensuring that everyone feels heard and valued.

4. Align on Expectations and Goals

Alignment is where clarity and collaboration converge. Leaders and teams must work together to set clear expectations and establish shared goals. This also includes agreeing to a timeline—a key point of accountability. This step ensures everyone is moving in the same direction, reducing confusion and fostering accountability.

5. Provide Feedback

Feedback—communication back from the people who are receiving information—is the loop that completes the process. Constructive, timely feedback helps individuals grow, reinforces alignment, and keeps communication flowing. Leaders who provide clear, actionable feedback create an environment where improvement and learning are part of the culture. Feedback needs to be a balance of positive reinforcement and constructive criticism; neither should dominate consistently.

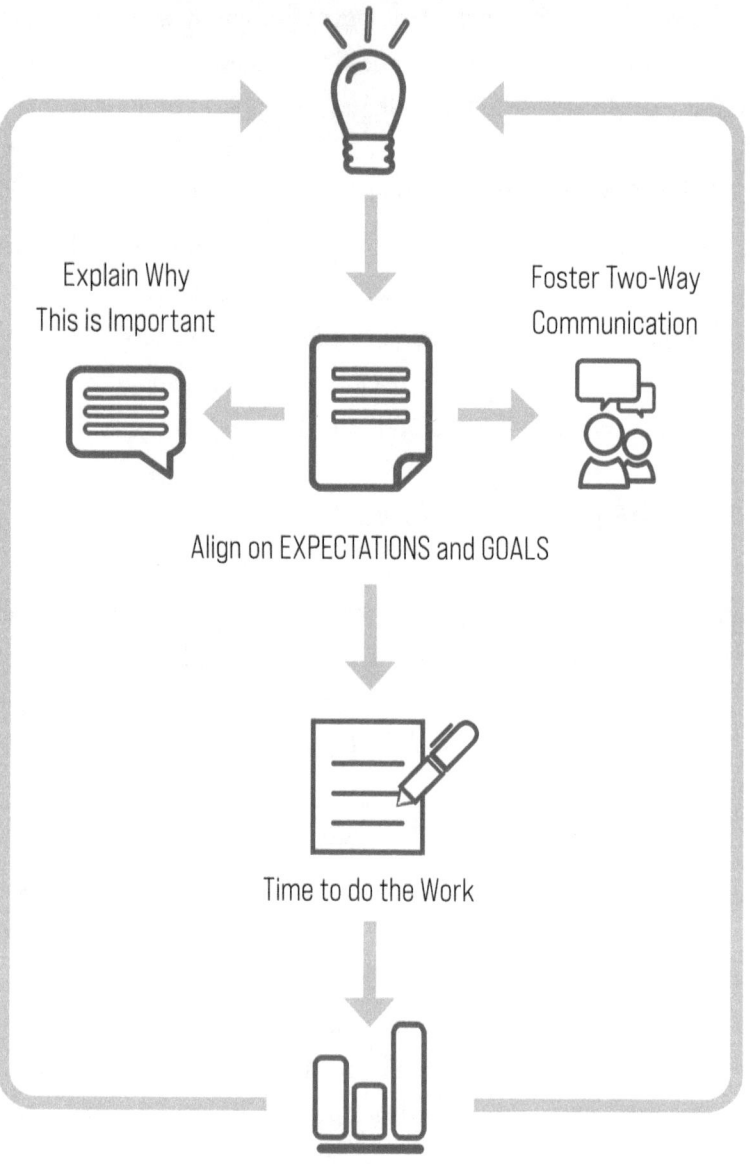

Each step in this model builds momentum, moving teams from understanding and collaboration to actionable alignment. The process fosters transparency at every stage, ensuring employees feel connected to their work and empowered to succeed. Remember that it might take multiple communication loops before you reach a successful outcome.

The transparent communication cycle depicts a model of the flow in organizational dynamics. As you implement this model in your organization, be consistent. Apply each step in the same basic way each time you use it. Transparent communication isn't just a one-time effort—it's a continuous practice that builds trust and strengthens teams.

HOW TO FOSTER TRANSPARENT COMMUNICATION

Here are some key strategies for fostering transparent communication within your organization:

1. Create Open Channels for Feedback

One of the most effective ways to foster transparency is by creating regular opportunities for feedback. This could include team meetings, one-on-one check-ins, anonymous surveys, or even informal conversations. Ensure your team knows you're providing a safe space to express their thoughts and that their feedback is valued.

In Sarah's case, she implemented biweekly feedback sessions, which allowed her team to share their concerns openly. These sessions weren't just for airing grievances; they provided a structured opportunity to discuss what was working and what wasn't. Sarah took the feedback seriously, addressing issues head-on and making changes where necessary. This practice helped the team feel heard and encouraged more open dialogue in the future.

> **Practical Tip:** Establish regular feedback opportunities and be consistent. Remember to both give and request feedback regularly. Whether it's weekly meetings, monthly surveys, or quarterly reviews, make sure your team has a consistent way to share their thoughts.

2. Be Honest, Even When It's Difficult

Transparency requires honesty, especially during difficult times. When the news isn't good, it can be tempting to withhold information or sugarcoat the truth, but doing so only erodes trust. Your team needs to know that you're being upfront with them, even when the situation is challenging.

Ethan showed this during the Four-Fifty competitor crisis at Brightpath. Instead of pretending everything was fine or rushing to introduce their new product to the market, he communicated openly with his team. He acknowledged the threat they were facing and was clear about the steps they were taking to address it. By doing this, he maintained the trust he had built with his team, and they were more willing to rally around the company's efforts to respond to the crisis.

> **Practical Tip:** Practice honest communication, even when it's uncomfortable. If you're facing a difficult situation, let your team know what's happening and be clear about what you're doing to address it.

3. Clarify Expectations and Goals

A key element of transparent communication is ensuring that everyone understands what's expected of them. Don't assume they know just because you've told them once and they are nodding their head; ask them about their perception. Misalignment in expectations can lead to frustration, missed deadlines, and decreased performance. By clearly communicating goals, timelines, and responsibilities, you create a shared understanding that allows your team to work effectively.

A great example of this was Ethan's integration of *The Accountability Matrix* into the company's transparent communication strategy. By outlining clear expectations for each team member and aligning their individual goals with the company's broader objectives, he eliminated ambiguity and made it easier for the team to collaborate. The matrix wasn't just a performance tracker—it was a tool for fostering open communication about what needed to be done and how it should be achieved.

> **Practical Tip:** Make sure expectations are both clearly communicated and also understood. Hold regular check-ins to ensure that your team knows what's expected and feels empowered to ask questions when things aren't clear.

4. Encourage Open Dialogue, Not Just Top-Down Communication

Transparent communication involves creating an environment where ideas, concerns, and feedback flow both ways. Leaders must be open to receiving feedback just as much as they give it. When team members feel comfortable offering their thoughts and input, it leads to more innovative solutions and better decision-making.

At Brightpath, Sarah encouraged her team to share their ideas and offer feedback during the biweekly sessions, but she didn't stop there. She also sought feedback on her own performance and leadership, which helped her make adjustments and better support her team. This two-way communication built mutual respect and trust, making the team more cohesive and engaged.

> **Practical Tip:** Request feedback about your leadership. Show your team that you value their input by listening to their suggestions and acting on them when appropriate.

THE IMPACT OF TRANSPARENCY ON TEAM DYNAMICS

When communication is transparent, it strengthens relationships, boosts morale, and fosters accountability. Team members who know they can openly share their thoughts without fear of judgment are more likely to collaborate, take ownership of their work, and feel invested in the team's success.

Transparent communication also helps to address problems before they escalate. Minor issues, if left unspoken, can grow into major challenges. But when teams communicate openly, they can solve problems quickly and effectively. At Brightpath, introducing feedback loops allowed the marketing teams to identify and address roadblocks early rather than letting frustrations build up in silence. This led to smoother operations, higher productivity, and a more positive work environment.

PRACTICAL APPLICATIONS: HOW TO BUILD TRANSPARENT COMMUNICATION IN YOUR ORGANIZATION

1. Establish Regular Check-Ins

Implement regular one-on-one meetings or team check-ins where everyone can share updates, raise concerns, and ask questions. These check-ins should be consistent, allowing your team to expect and rely on them as a space for open dialogue.

2. Provide Multiple Avenues for Feedback

Not everyone feels comfortable speaking up in meetings, so it's important to offer multiple channels for feedback. This could include anonymous surveys, suggestion boxes, or one-on-one conversations. The key is to create options that work for unique personalities and communication styles.

3. Be Transparent About Decisions

When making important decisions, clearly explain how and why you made them. Explain the reasoning behind the changes, especially if they affect the team's day-to-day work. This level of transparency helps team members feel more connected to the decision-making process and reduces any sense of uncertainty.

4. Model the Behavior You Want to See

As a leader, your communication style sets the tone for the entire team. If you want your team to communicate openly, you need to model that behavior. Be honest, share information proactively, and be open to feedback. When your team sees you practicing transparency, they will follow your lead.

FINAL THOUGHT: TRANSPARENCY IS A TWO-WAY STREET

Transparent communication isn't just about leaders sharing information—it's about fostering an environment where open, honest dialogue flows in all directions. As a leader, it's your responsibility to create the conditions where this kind of communication can thrive. By establishing clear expectations, providing regular feedback opportunities, and being honest about challenges, you build a team that feels empowered, respected, and aligned with the organization's goals.

In every chapter of the Brightpath story, opaque communications lead to disaster, and open communications are rewarded. Victor and Jennifer set the whole crisis in motion when they hid their financial mistakes. This is an accurate description of corporate activity today: transparent communication yields dividends. The episodes featuring open communication by Ethan, Leah, Rajiv, Emma, and Sarah all reflect events that my colleagues and I have encountered in real-world situations.

In the next chapter, we'll explore how accountability builds on the foundation of trust and communication, helping leaders foster a culture of ownership and responsibility within their teams.

ACCOUNTABILITY BUILT ON TRUST

People often misunderstand accountability. It's not about placing blame or creating fear with harsh consequences for failure; it's about taking ownership of actions, decisions, and results. True accountability, however, cannot be forced—it has to be built on a foundation of trust. Without trust, accountability quickly turns into micromanagement, which can stifle creativity, breed resentment, and erode the very culture leaders work so hard to build.

Accountability built on trust is a shared responsibility, where leaders and team members alike hold each other to high standards of performance, behavior, and integrity. This shared responsibility creates an environment where people feel safe owning their successes and their mistakes, knowing that they'll be supported throughout their process of improvement.

THE LINK BETWEEN TRUST AND ACCOUNTABILITY

Accountability and trust are deeply intertwined. Trust provides the psychological safety necessary for people to take risks, admit mistakes, and ask for help. Psychological safety is the creation of an atmosphere where people know there will be no repercussions for expressing their ideas and opinions. Without trust, people may avoid accountability out of fear—fear of being blamed, punished, or singled out.

Consider how Ethan approached accountability at Brightpath. After Greg's departure, one of his first major initiatives was to rebuild trust within the organization. This was essential before introducing any systems of accountability. Ethan knew that without a foundation of trust, his efforts to create a culture of accountability would appear punitive or controlling.

By fostering trust first—through transparency, empathy, and consistent communication—Ethan could implement *The Accountability Matrix* effectively. The matrix had metrics that went beyond financial or operational performance. It measured how people were supporting one another, how leaders were providing the resources their teams needed, and how everyone was working toward shared goals. This created a culture where people embraced, rather than feared, accountability.

A complete Accountability Matrix template is available in the tools and resources chapter at the end of this book.

CREATING A CULTURE OF ACCOUNTABILITY

Creating a culture of accountability isn't about enforcing rules or setting strict deadlines. It's about fostering ownership, where team members feel responsible for their own work and for contributing to the success of the team. Here are a few strategies for building accountability that is grounded in trust:

1. Set Clear Expectations

Accountability begins with clarity. If people don't know what's expected of them, it's impossible for them to take ownership of their work. As a leader, it's your responsibility to ensure that every team member understands their role, their responsibilities, and how their work contributes to the broader organizational goals.

At Brightpath, *The Accountability Matrix* provided clear expectations for each team member. It explained how every task aligned with the company's strategic objectives. By providing this clarity, Sarah empowered her team to take ownership of their work and feel accountable for its success.

> **Practical Tip:** Clearly define roles and responsibilities for each team member. Regularly check in with each team member to confirm their alignment with team goals and individual expectations.

2. Lead by Example

Accountability starts with the leader. If you want your team to hold themselves accountable, you need to show that same level of accountability in your actions. This means being open about your own mistakes, following through on your commitments, and taking responsibility for your decisions.

Ethan consistently showed accountability at Brightpath. When things didn't go according to plan—whether it was a delayed product launch or a tough decision—he didn't deflect responsibility. He owned his role in the situation and worked with the team to find solutions. By doing so, he showed that accountability was a shared value, not something to fear.

> **Practical Tip:** Be transparent about your own accountability as a leader. Share your decision-making process, acknowledge your mistakes, and model the behavior you want to see in your team.

3. Encourage Open Feedback

Accountability isn't a one-way street. As you hold your team accountable, you allow your team to hold you accountable as well. Your role in the process includes inviting feedback from them and taking what they tell you seriously. Even if it's not accurate, they're expressing a real reaction that indicates a real issue you must address. Doing this regularly creates a culture where accountability is a mutual expectation. This kind of environment empowers everyone to speak up, share concerns, and work together to improve.

At Brightpath, Sarah's biweekly feedback sessions weren't just for team members to voice their concerns; they were also an opportunity for the team to give feedback on her leadership. By opening herself up to feedback, Sarah showed that accountability applied to everyone, including herself. Their mutual accountability strengthened the trust within the team and encouraged more honest, open communication.

> **Practical Tip:** Create regular opportunities for your team to provide feedback on your leadership. Encourage them to hold you accountable in the same way you hold them accountable.

4. Focus on Solutions, Not Blame

Accountability should never be about blame or punishment. Instead, it should be about finding solutions and learning from mistakes. When a team member doesn't meet expectations, the conversation shouldn't center on what went wrong. Instead, use the time to focus on how to move forward. By focusing on solutions, leaders create a culture where people feel safe to admit their mistakes and take responsibility for improving.

Ethan's approach to accountability at Brightpath was solution-focused. When a project fell behind, or a mistake was made, Ethan always focused the conversation on fixing the problem and ensuring it wouldn't happen again. We saw this in the quality crisis episode when he mediated the tension between Emma and Greg. His approach encouraged team members to own their mistakes without fear of reprisal, knowing that the focus would be on how to improve rather than on who to blame.

> **Practical Tip:** When mistakes happen, avoid pointing fingers. Collaborate with your team to identify solutions and develop a plan. This fosters accountability without fear.

HOW ACCOUNTABILITY DRIVES TEAM PERFORMANCE

A culture of accountability doesn't just benefit individuals—it drives the entire team's performance. When everyone feels responsible for their work and for the success of the team, collaboration improves, innovation increases, and problems get solved faster. Accountability, when rooted in trust, also encourages people to take ownership of their growth and development, leading to higher engagement and long-term success.

At Brightpath, implementing *The Accountability Matrix* had a noticeable impact on team performance. By setting clear expectations and encouraging open communication, the team became more aligned and more highly motivated to deliver their best work, too. Instead of fearing accountability, team members embraced it, knowing their contributions mattered and their leaders supported them.

PRACTICAL APPLICATIONS: HOW TO BUILD ACCOUNTABILITY IN YOUR ORGANIZATION

1. Define Clear Expectations and Goals

Make sure that every team member understands their role, responsibilities, and how their work contributes to the overall goals of the team. Track progress and ensure alignment with organizational objectives using tools like *The Accountability Matrix*. Accountability matrices can be as simple as the example below or as complex as the example provided in the tools and resources chapter.

SIMPLE ACCOUNTABILITY MATRIX EXAMPLE

	Director	Warehouse Manager	Clerk
Inventory	Informed	Responsible	Informed
Shipping	Informed	Responsible	N/A
Returns	N/A	Informed	Responsible

2. Create a Feedback Culture

Encourage open, honest feedback between team members and leaders. Make feedback a regular part of your team's workflow and ensure that it's constructive and solution-oriented.

3. Model Accountability as a Leader

Demonstrate accountability in your own actions. Share your decision-making process, admit when you've made mistakes, and follow through on your commitments. This sets the tone for the rest of the team.

4. Celebrate Accountability and Ownership

Recognize and celebrate when team members take ownership of their work and hold themselves accountable. Value and encourage accountability through public recognition, private conversations, or team celebrations.

FINAL THOUGHT: ACCOUNTABILITY STRENGTHENS TRUST AND CULTURE

Accountability, when built on trust, becomes a powerful force for good within any organization. It encourages ownership, fosters collaboration, and creates a culture where people feel empowered to take responsibility for their actions. As a leader, your role is to create the conditions where accountability thrives—not through fear or punishment, but through trust, transparency, and mutual respect.

In the next chapter, we'll explore how servant leadership deepens these principles by focusing on serving others and fostering growth, both for individuals and for the team.

SERVANT LEADERSHIP: LEADING BY SERVING OTHERS

People often view leadership as power—the ability to make decisions, influence others, and drive results. But what if we flipped the script? What if leadership was less about exercising power over others and more about serving them? That's the essence of **servant leadership**: putting the needs of your team first, helping them grow, and empowering them to succeed.

At its core, servant leadership is about trust, humility, and a deep commitment to the development of others. Rather than focusing on your own success, you focus on the success of those around you, creating an environment where people feel valued, supported, and inspired to give their best. When leaders serve, teams thrive.

WHAT IS SERVANT LEADERSHIP?

Servant leadership is a leadership philosophy that emphasizes the leader's role in service to their team. Robert K. Greenleaf coined the term in 1970, and it challenges the traditional, hierarchical view of leadership. Instead of using power to control, a servant leader uses influence and support to guide their team.

Some key principles of servant leadership include:

- **Service First:** The leader's main role is to serve others. This contrasts with leaders who seek power for personal gain.

- **Listening and Empathy:** Actively listening to your team, not just hearing their words, but understanding their concerns and ideas.

- **Awareness and Foresight:** Self-awareness, situational awareness, and the ability to anticipate future challenges and opportunities, making proactive decisions that benefit the team.

- **Empowerment:** Giving your team the tools, resources, and authority they need to succeed.

- **Community Building:** Creating a sense of belonging and shared purpose within the team.

THE IMPACT OF SERVANT LEADERSHIP

When leaders focus on serving their team rather than commanding them, it creates a powerful ripple effect. Trust deepens, collaboration improves, and people feel more engaged and motivated. Servant leaders build long-lasting commitment and foster a culture where everyone is encouraged to grow.

At Brightpath, Sarah exemplified servant leadership in the way she approached the marketing department's transformation. Instead of coming in with a top-down, directive approach, she listened to her team. She held one-on-one meetings, seeking to understand their frustrations and concerns. Instead of dictating solutions, she empowered the team members to develop their own ideas for improvement.

By serving her team's needs and helping them take ownership of their growth, Sarah earned their trust and respect. The team became more collaborative, more creative, and ultimately more successful. Sarah's leadership wasn't about being the loudest voice in the room—it was about amplifying the voices of others.

HOW TO PRACTICE SERVANT LEADERSHIP

1. Listen First

Servant leadership starts with listening. Before making decisions, take time to listen to your team's input, concerns, and ideas. Active listening shows you value their perspectives and creates an environment where people feel safe sharing openly.

> **Practical Tip:** In meetings, try to ask questions more often than you give answers. Encourage team members to speak up and listen without interrupting. Take notes and reflect on what's been said before offering your own thoughts.

2. Empower Your Team

Servant leaders don't just delegate tasks—they delegate authority. Empowering your team means giving them the tools, resources, and autonomy to take ownership of their work. This also means trusting them to make decisions and supporting them even when they make mistakes.

> **Practical Tip:** Instead of micromanaging, set clear goals and provide the resources your team needs to be successful. Then, step back and give your team the space to solve problems their way. If they stumble, offer guidance, not criticism.

3. Support Personal and Professional Growth

Servant leaders dedicate themselves to the growth of their team members. This means providing opportunities for learning, mentoring, and professional development. When your team knows that you're invested in their personal and professional success, they're more likely to trust and follow you.

> **Practical Tip:** Regularly check in with each team member about their career goals. Provide opportunities for growth via training, mentorship, and challenging new projects. Celebrate their successes and provide constructive feedback for continuous improvement.

4. Show Empathy and Compassion

Servant leaders understand that their team members are not just workers—they're people with their own challenges, fears, and aspirations. Empathy allows you to connect with your team on a human level, building trust and deepening relationships.

> **Practical Tip:** When a team member is struggling, take the time to understand what they're going through. Offer support, whether it's a flexible schedule, additional resources, or simply a listening ear. Minor acts of compassion go a long way in building trust.

5. Lead by Example

Servant leaders model the behaviors they want to see in their team. Whether it's showing humility, owning mistakes, or working collaboratively, your actions as a leader set the tone for the entire team.

> **Practical Tip:** If you want your team to collaborate, show them how it's done. Work alongside them, share credit for successes, and be open about your own areas for improvement. When you lead by example, your team is more likely to follow.

THE BENEFITS OF SERVANT LEADERSHIP

- **Higher Engagement:** When leaders focus on serving their team, employees feel more engaged, motivated, and loyal. Employees are more likely to work harder if they feel appreciated and supported.

- **Increased Innovation:** Empowering team members to take ownership of their work leads to more creative problem-solving and innovation. When people feel safe to experiment and take risks, they're more likely to come up with breakthrough ideas.

- **Stronger Trust:** Servant leadership deepens trust between leaders and their teams. When leaders put the needs of others first, it shows they care about the team's success as much as their own.

- **Long-Term Success:** Servant leadership isn't about short-term gains—it's about building a sustainable culture of collaboration, trust, and growth. Teams led by servant leaders perform better over the long run because they're more cohesive and resilient.

PRACTICAL APPLICATIONS: HOW TO LEAD BY SERVING OTHERS

1. Assess Your Leadership Style

Take a moment to reflect on your leadership approach. Are you primarily focused on directing and managing, or are you empowering your team to take ownership? Identify areas where you can shift from a command-and-control approach to one that's more focused on serving and supporting.

2. Create Opportunities for Growth

Look for ways to develop your team's skills and abilities. Offer mentorship, provide resources for learning, and challenge your team with new opportunities that stretch their capabilities. Encourage them to take risks and support them when they do.

3. Recognize and Celebrate Contributions

Servant leaders know that success is a team effort. Make it a habit to recognize the contributions of your team members—both big and small. Whether through public recognition, personal notes, or team celebrations, showing appreciation for your team's hard work builds morale and strengthens trust.

4. Foster a Collaborative Environment

Servant leadership thrives in a collaborative environment. Encourage your team to work together, share ideas, and solve problems as a group. As a leader, facilitate collaboration by creating spaces where team members feel safe to contribute.

FINAL THOUGHT: SERVANT LEADERSHIP IS A LONG-TERM INVESTMENT

Servant leadership isn't a quick fix. It's a long-term investment in the growth and success of your team. By putting others first, you build a culture where trust, collaboration, and innovation flourish. In the process, you create a team that's not only more effective, but more engaged and fulfilled.

In the next chapter, we'll explore how to navigate crises as a leader and the role transparency, communication, and accountability play in leading through uncertain times.

LEADING THROUGH CRISIS

No matter how well-prepared a leader is, crises are inevitable. Whether it's an unexpected market disruption, a financial setback, or internal conflict, every leader will face moments of uncertainty that test their leadership. In these moments, how you lead will determine not just how the organization survives the crisis, but how it thrives afterward.

Leading through a crisis requires a balance of transparency, calm decision-making, and a focus on both short-term and long-term solutions. More importantly, a crisis gives leaders an opportunity to reinforce the values of trust, communication, and accountability they have cultivated.

THE ROLE OF LEADERSHIP DURING CRISIS

A crisis often creates anxiety, uncertainty, and confusion. People naturally look to their leaders for guidance, clarity, and reassurance. This is when leadership becomes most crucial. During times of crisis, leaders need to:

1. **Stay calm and composed:** The way a leader reacts to a crisis sets the tone for the entire organization.

2. **Communicate openly and frequently:** Clear, consistent communication can ease fears and provide direction.

3. **Make decisions confidently:** Leaders must assess the situation quickly and make decisions, even when all the information isn't available.

4. **Maintain accountability and integrity:** Even in moments of chaos, leaders must remain accountable for their actions and keep the organization's core values intact.

Ethan faced one of these pivotal moments at Brightpath during the competitor crisis. When the rival Four-Fifty launched a faster, cheaper, and more advanced product, many of Brightpath's long-standing clients reconsidered their loyalty. Contracts were on the line, and the company's future seemed uncertain. Ethan knew that his response would determine whether the team crumbled under pressure or came together to overcome the challenge.

STAYING CALM AND FOCUSED

One of the most important traits of a leader during a crisis is the ability to stay calm under pressure. In a crisis, emotions can run high, and it can be challenging not to let fear or frustration take over. Leaders who remain calm help their teams stay grounded and focused, ensuring that the situation doesn't spiral out of control.

At Brightpath, Ethan set the tone for the company by remaining composed throughout the crisis. Instead of panicking or rushing to implement a quick fix, he took a step back, assessed the situation, and focused on finding the right solution. He insisted others do the same. His calm demeanor reassured the team that they could weather the storm.

> **Practical Tip:** When faced with a crisis, take a moment to breathe and assess the situation before reacting. Maintain a level-headed approach and be mindful of how your emotions and actions will influence your team. By staying calm, you create an environment where others can think clearly and contribute to problem-solving.

COMMUNICATING WITH TRANSPARENCY

In times of crisis, transparent communication becomes even more critical. People need to understand what's happening, how the organization is responding, and what role they play in overcoming the challenge. Without clear communication, rumors and misunderstandings can spread, further destabilizing the team.

Ethan knew that Brightpath's team needed clear and honest updates about the situation with their competitor. Instead of hiding the threat or downplaying the challenges, he communicated openly with the entire company. He acknowledged the risks, but he also provided reassurance by outlining the steps the company was taking to respond. His transparency built trust, showing the team they were in this together.

> **Practical Tip:** During a crisis, keep communication frequent and transparent. Even when you don't have all the

answers, it's important to be upfront with your team. Share what you know, what you're doing to address the situation, and what role the team plays in resolving it. This transparency will help maintain trust and focus.

DECISIVE DECISION-MAKING

One of the biggest challenges of leading through a crisis is the need to make decisions quickly, often with incomplete information. Delaying decisions out of fear of making the wrong choice can paralyze the team and exacerbate the situation. However, it's equally important not to rush into hasty decisions that might have unintended consequences.

At Brightpath, Ethan and the executive team faced a tough decision: should they rush the launch of a new product to compete with their rival, or should they stick to their commitment to quality and risk losing clients in the short term? After careful consideration, Ethan chose the latter. He knew that rushing the product launch would damage their reputation in the long run. Instead, he communicated with clients about their commitment to maintaining quality and reassured them that the product, when launched, would surpass expectations.

> **Practical Tip:** In a crisis, make decisions based on a balance of immediate needs and long-term impact. When faced with tough choices, involve your team in the decision-making process and gather as much relevant information as possible. Once you make a decision, communicate it clearly, support it, and confidently lead your team.

MAINTAINING ACCOUNTABILITY

Crises can make it tempting to let accountability slip. Uncertainty might tempt leaders to avoid accountability and lower their standards to reduce pressure. However, during a crisis, maintaining accountability is essential to keeping the team aligned and focused on the right actions.

A good example of this was Ethan's decision to maintain Brightpath's commitment to quality during the competitor crisis. Even though the company was under pressure to act quickly, Ethan held the team accountable to their values, reminding them that sacrificing quality would only hurt them in the long run.

> **Practical Tip:** During a crisis, stay true to the core values and standards of your organization. Hold yourself and your team accountable for actions and decisions. By maintaining high standards, you help the team stay focused on long-term success rather than short-term panic.

LEADING WITH EMPATHY

In a crisis, emotions run high. People may feel anxious, overwhelmed, or fearful about the future. As a leader, it's important to acknowledge these emotions and lead with empathy. Understanding and addressing your team's concerns helps them feel supported, and it reinforces the trust they have in you.

During Brightpath's crisis, Ethan made it a point to connect with team members individually, asking about their concerns and how the situation was affecting them. He wasn't just focused on the business. He demonstrated that he cared about how the crisis affected his people. This empathy helped the team stay motivated and committed to finding solutions, even in a difficult time.

> **Practical Tip:** Take time to check in with your team during a crisis. Ask how they're feeling, listen to their concerns, and provide emotional support as needed. Showing empathy strengthens your team's connection to you and helps them navigate challenges with greater resilience.

THE BENEFITS OF STRONG LEADERSHIP DURING A CRISIS

Crisis leadership isn't just about survival—it's about coming out stronger on the other side. Teams that navigate crises with strong leadership often become more cohesive, more innovative, and more resilient. They learn to trust one another, to work together under pressure, and to stay focused on long-term success.

At Brightpath, the crisis ultimately brought the team closer together. Ethan's calm, transparent leadership helped them not only weather the storm but emerge with a renewed sense of purpose and collaboration. The lessons learned during the crisis became part of Brightpath's culture, preparing the team to handle future challenges with confidence.

PRACTICAL APPLICATIONS: HOW TO LEAD THROUGH CRISIS

1. Create a Crisis Plan

While you can't predict every crisis, you can prepare for the unexpected. Create a crisis response plan that outlines key steps for communication, decision-making, and accountability. Make sure your team understands their roles and responsibilities in times of crisis.

2. Keep Communication Open

Ensure that your communication channels remain open during a crisis. Schedule regular updates, even if there's not much new information to share. Keeping the team informed will help reduce uncertainty and keep everyone aligned.

3. Delegate Responsibility

In a crisis, you can't handle everything yourself. Delegate responsibilities to trusted team members, giving them the authority to make decisions within their areas. Empowering your team to take ownership of their roles will keep the organization moving forward.

4. Reflect After the Crisis

Following a crisis, review successes and areas for improvement with your team. Discuss the lessons learned and how the organization can better prepare for future challenges. This reflection not only improves crisis response but also strengthens team cohesion.

FINAL THOUGHT: CRISES AS LEADERSHIP OPPORTUNITIES

Crises, while challenging, are also leadership opportunities. They test your ability to remain calm, communicate transparently, and maintain accountability under pressure. How you lead during a crisis will define your legacy—not just in how you manage the situation, but in how you strengthen your team and build resilience for the future.

In the next chapter, we'll examine how leaders can foster innovation within their teams and create a culture that encourages creative problem-solving and forward-thinking solutions.

FOSTERING INNOVATION THROUGH LEADERSHIP

Innovation is the lifeblood of any successful organization. Whether you're introducing a groundbreaking product, optimizing internal processes, or finding creative ways to serve customers, innovation keeps companies competitive and helps them grow. But innovation doesn't just happen—it requires intentional leadership that fosters an environment where creativity, experimentation, and calculated risk-taking can thrive.

As a leader, you should encourage creativity, experimentation, and new ways of thinking for your team. When leaders model curiosity and embrace change, they inspire their teams to do the same.

THE ROLE OF LEADERSHIP IN INNOVATION

People often consider product teams or research and development departments as the domain of innovation. However, we can see true innovation in every part of an organization, from customer service and operations to marketing. And it starts with leadership.

As a leader, you set the tone for innovation within your organization. If you foster a culture that encourages experimentation and views failure as a learning opportunity, your team will be more likely to take risks and explore new ideas. However, if you discourage or overly control innovation, creativity suffers, and the organization stagnates.

Emma's leadership in the product team at Brightpath provides a simple example of how leaders can foster innovation. Faced with pressure from competitors, Emma had to push her team to innovate without sacrificing quality. She created an environment where the team felt empowered to experiment, collaborate, and test new ideas—all while maintaining their commitment to excellence.

HOW TO FOSTER INNOVATION WITHIN YOUR TEAM

1. Encourage Experimentation

Innovation thrives in a setting in which team members can experiment without fear of failure. Encouraging experimentation doesn't mean abandoning standards or pursuing reckless ideas—it means creating space for creative problem-solving and calculated risks.

At Brightpath, Emma encouraged her product team to try alternative approaches and test ideas, even if they didn't always succeed. She introduced rapid prototyping sessions, where the team could brainstorm and quickly test ideas. This allowed them to explore new solutions without over-committing resources to any one concept. Some ideas didn't work, but the team learned from each iteration and improved over time.

> **Practical Tip:** Create opportunities for your team to experiment, such as innovation sprints or brainstorming

sessions. Set aside time for idea generation and encourage your team to explore different possibilities. Let them know that failure is part of the process and that every experiment—successful or not—is a learning experience.

2. Promote Cross-Department Collaboration

Some of the best innovations come from unexpected places. By encouraging collaboration across departments, you can generate fresh ideas and new perspectives that might not emerge within siloed teams. Different departments often have different ways of thinking, and bringing those perspectives together can lead to breakthrough solutions.

At Brightpath, Emma worked closely with Sarah in marketing and Leah in operations to ensure that product innovation wasn't just limited to the product team. By involving other departments in the early stages of product development, Emma's team gained valuable insights that improved the final product. This cross-department collaboration also helped the company align its efforts toward a common goal, increasing efficiency and innovation throughout the organization.

> **Practical Tip:** Facilitate collaboration between teams by organizing cross-functional meetings or task forces. Bring together people from different departments to work on key challenges or projects and encourage them to share their insights and expertise.

3. Provide the Right Resources

Innovation requires resources—whether it's time, tools, or training. Routine tasks and lack of access to technology and skills limit your team's ability to innovate. As a leader, it's your responsibility to remove barriers and provide the resources that allow your team to explore new ideas and implement creative solutions.

Emma recognized early on that her team needed access to better tools to support their product development goals, especially under tight deadlines. She invested in advanced prototyping processes and ensured that the team had the time and space to focus on innovation without being overwhelmed by day-to-day operations. By providing the right resources, she empowered her team to push the boundaries of what they could achieve.

> **Practical Tip:** Assess the resources your team needs to innovate. Are there tools, training, or additional personnel that could help them experiment more effectively? Invest in what they need to succeed and remove any obstacles that may hinder their ability to think creatively.

4. Embrace a Continuous Learning Mindset

The hallmark of a learning mindset is not a onetime effort. It is a continuous process and requires an ongoing cycle of growth and refinement. The leader's role is to identify areas for improvement, take action to develop new skills, and then evaluate their progress through reflection and feedback. This cycle repeats as new challenges arise, ensuring leaders stay adaptable and relevant in a changing environment. Each stage of learning builds on the last, creating a momentum that fosters innovation and resilience. By modeling this cycle, leaders set the tone for their teams, encouraging a culture where learning and growth are valued at every level of the organization.

At Brightpath, Ethan regularly encouraged his team to seek new information and stay ahead of industry trends. He sponsored ongoing training and professional development opportunities, enabling team members to stay sharp and innovative. This learning mindset became embedded in the company culture, driving a constant push toward improvement and creative problem-solving.

> **Practical Tip:** Promote a learning culture by encouraging team members to attend workshops, conferences, and training programs. Stay up-to-date on industry trends and share insights with your team. Demonstrate your own commitment to continuous learning by seeking new knowledge and sharing it with your team.

BALANCING INNOVATION WITH ACCOUNTABILITY

One challenge leaders face is balancing innovation with accountability. While it's important to encourage creativity and experimentation, it's equally important to maintain accountability and ensure that innovation aligns with the organization's goals.

At Brightpath, Emma set clear objectives for the product team. She allowed them the freedom to experiment, but she also ensured every new idea aligned with the company's broader goals. By establishing guardrails and tracking progress, Emma ensured that the team's innovative efforts were both productive and purposeful.

> **Practical Tip:** Provide your team with clear objectives and guidelines for innovation. Encourage creativity within the framework of the company's goals and values. This ensures the alignment of innovation with the organization's mission, while preserving creative freedom.

THE BENEFITS OF A CULTURE OF INNOVATION

- **Increased Engagement:** When team members feel empowered to contribute ideas and explore creative solutions, they're more engaged in their work. Innovation fuels excitement and ownership, which leads to higher morale and better performance.

- **Better Problem-Solving:** Innovative teams are better equipped to solve complex problems. By fostering an environment that encourages creativity, you empower your team to tackle challenges from different angles and develop more effective solutions.

- **Sustained Growth:** Innovation is essential for long-term growth. Companies that continuously innovate are better positioned to adapt to market changes, meet growing customer needs, and stay ahead of competitors.

PRACTICAL APPLICATIONS: HOW TO FOSTER INNOVATION AS A LEADER

1. Encourage Risk-Taking

Let your team know that it's okay to take calculated risks. Innovation requires stepping outside of the status quo, and not every idea will succeed. Foster an environment that celebrates experimentation, even when it doesn't yield immediate results.

2. Create Innovation Challenges

Organize innovation challenges or hackathons where your team can focus on solving specific problems or exploring new opportunities.

These focused efforts can generate breakthrough ideas while fostering team collaboration.

3. Recognize and Reward Innovation

Celebrate innovative ideas and solutions, even if they don't immediately lead to implementation. Publicly acknowledge team members who contribute creative solutions and celebrate their efforts to foster a culture of innovation.

4. Foster Curiosity

Encourage team members to ask questions, explore new technologies, and stay curious about what's happening in the industry. Curiosity drives innovation, so make learning and exploration part of your team's routine.

FINAL THOUGHT: INNOVATION AS A LEADERSHIP IMPERATIVE

Fostering innovation isn't just a nice-to-have—it's a leadership imperative. In a world where industries and technologies change rapidly, innovation is essential for staying competitive and achieving long-term success. As a leader, your role is to create the conditions where innovation can thrive, empowering your team to explore new ideas, take risks, and push boundaries.

In the next chapter, we'll explore how leaders can navigate tough decisions, especially when those decisions affect the future of the team or the organization.

NAVIGATING DIFFICULT DECISIONS

Leadership often requires making decisions that are uncomfortable, complex, or unpopular. Whether it's letting go of a high-performing but toxic team member, making cuts in challenging times, or choosing between competing priorities, the ability to make tough decisions is a defining trait of effective leadership.

Difficult decisions test your principles as a leader. They force you to balance short-term needs with long-term goals, consider the well-being of individuals versus the organization, and sometimes make choices that won't please everyone. But when approached with integrity and clarity, even the hardest decisions can strengthen trust, accountability, and your leadership credibility.

THE CHALLENGE OF DIFFICULT DECISIONS

Difficult decisions often involve trade-offs. Many times, there's no "perfect" option—each choice has pros and cons, and leaders must weigh the outcomes carefully. These situations are often complicated by emotional factors, conflicting interests, and the pressure to act quickly.

One of the most difficult decisions Ethan faced at Brightpath was letting go of Greg, a high-performing but toxic leader. Greg consistently delivered results, but his behavior eroded trust and undermined the company's culture. Ethan knew that keeping Greg would yield short-term benefits, but would ultimately damage the team in the long run. The decision to let Greg go wasn't easy, but it was necessary to preserve Brightpath's values of trust and collaboration.

PRINCIPLES FOR MAKING DIFFICULT DECISIONS

When faced with tough decisions, leaders must rely on a set of guiding principles to help navigate the complexities. Here are several key principles to keep in mind:

1. Align with Core Values

Every decision you make as a leader should align with the core values of your organization. Even when a decision is difficult, if it upholds the values you've built your organization around, it will ultimately reinforce trust and consistency.

In Ethan's case, the decision to let Greg go aligned with Brightpath's commitment to trust and accountability. By staying true to these values, Ethan demonstrated to the rest of the team that the culture they were building mattered more than any one individual's performance.

> **Practical Tip:** Before making a difficult decision, reflect on your organization's core values. Ask yourself whether

the decision supports those values or undermines them. When decisions align with your values, they reinforce your leadership and strengthen the organization's culture.

2. Consider Long-Term Impact

Tough decisions often require you to balance short-term benefits with long-term consequences. While the immediate effects of a decision might be challenging, consider how it will affect your team, your organization, and your leadership in the future.

Ethan could have kept Greg on the team for the sake of short-term results, but he recognized that doing so would undermine the long-term health of the company. By making the difficult decision to prioritize culture over performance, he protected Brightpath's future and its values.

> **Practical Tip:** When faced with a difficult decision, take a long-term view. Ask yourself how the decision will affect the organization's health and success in six months, a year, or five years down the road.

3. Be Transparent and Honest

One of the most important aspects of making difficult decisions is how you communicate them to those who are most affected, as well as to the company as a whole. Transparency builds trust, even when the decision is unpopular. Clearly explain the reasoning behind the decision, the factors you considered, and the expected outcomes. Your team may not always agree with your decision, but they'll respect you more if you're open and honest.

Ethan was transparent with Greg about the issues involved. He clarified why accountability and trust were two of the company-wide focus areas and gave Greg a chance to change his views before making the decision to fire him. He was also candid with the executive team and the board chair about why Greg had to go. He didn't soften the blow or cover up the reasons—he communicated the decision clearly and explained how it aligned with the company's values. This level of transparency helped the team understand the bigger picture and reinforced the importance of trust and accountability.

> **Practical Tip:** Communicate your decisions openly and honestly. Provide context, explain your reasoning, and be upfront about any challenges or trade-offs. Your transparency will build credibility, even in difficult times.

4. Seek Input but Own the Decision

Gathering input from others is essential for making informed decisions, but as a leader, the responsibility ultimately falls on you. Involving your team in the decision-making process helps you understand different perspectives and ensures that you're making a well-rounded choice. However, you must take full responsibility for the decision once it's made.

Before deciding to let Greg go, Ethan consulted with Tanya. However, Ethan knew that the final decision rested with him, and once he made it, he took full responsibility for its execution.

> **Practical Tip:** Involve your team in the decision-making process, especially for difficult decisions that impact them directly. Seek diverse perspectives, but be prepared to take ownership of the eventual choice and its consequences.

5. Balance Empathy with Accountability

When making difficult decisions, it's important to balance empathy with accountability. While leaders must show compassion and understanding, they must also hold individuals accountable for their actions or performance.

Ethan's decision to let Greg go was not made without empathy for him and his team. He understood the implications of the decision for Greg's career, but he also knew that Greg's behavior was damaging the team. Ethan balanced compassion for Greg's situation with accountability for the greater good of the company.

> **Practical Tip:** Approach difficult decisions with empathy, but don't let compassion prevent you from holding people accountable. Offer support where possible and ensure that decisions serve the best interests of the team and organization.

HOW TO NAVIGATE DECISIONS THAT DIRECTLY IMPACT PEOPLE

Some of the toughest decisions leaders make are those that affect individuals directly—whether it's layoffs, performance-based dismissals, or restructuring. Making these decisions and communicating them to those affected carries strong emotional weight and demands careful handling.

1. Have Direct Conversations

When a difficult decision affects an individual, it's important to have a direct and honest conversation with them. Avoid sugarcoating the issue or hiding behind vague language. Be clear about the reasons for the decision and show them respect by offering a straightforward explanation.

2. Offer Support

Provide support to those affected by the decision. Whether it's offering severance, career counseling, or a letter of recommendation, showing that you care about their well-being can make a difficult situation more bearable.

3. Be Consistent

Ensure that your decision-making process is consistent and based on clear criteria. Inconsistent decisions can lead to feelings of unfairness and erode trust within the team.

THE BENEFITS OF MAKING TOUGH DECISIONS WITH INTEGRITY

When leaders make difficult decisions with integrity, they build trust, reinforce organizational values, and strengthen their leadership credibility. Even when a decision is unpopular, if it's made with honesty, empathy, and alignment with core values, it will ultimately lead to greater respect and stronger relationships within the team.

Ethan's decision to let Greg go was hard, but it demonstrated to the rest of the team that no one was above the company's values of trust, accountability, and transparent communication. Unlike the decisions to remove Victor and Jennifer, it also showed that Ethan was willing to own these tough decisions and accept accountability for them. By making a tough decision with integrity, Ethan reinforced the importance of culture and set a precedent for future leadership decisions.

PRACTICAL APPLICATIONS: HOW TO NAVIGATE DIFFICULT DECISIONS

1. Develop a Decision-Making Framework

Create a decision-making framework that aligns with your organization's values. This framework should help guide you through tough choices by focusing on long-term impact, fairness, and alignment with the company's mission.

2. Involve Your Leadership Team

When faced with difficult decisions, involve your leadership team in the process. Gather their input, consider their perspectives, and ensure that they feel heard. This collaborative approach leads to better decision-making and helps build alignment across the team.

3. Own the Outcome

Once you make a decision, take full responsibility for its execution and outcome. Don't pass the blame if things don't go as planned. Your ability to own difficult decisions strengthens your leadership credibility and builds trust with your team.

4. Evaluate the Impact

After making a difficult decision, take time to evaluate its impact. Evaluate what succeeded, what could have been improved, and the decision's impact on the organization. Use these insights to improve future decision-making processes.

FINAL THOUGHT: LEADERSHIP IS DEFINED BY DIFFICULT DECISIONS

Leadership isn't defined by easy choices, but by the tough calls demanding courage, integrity, and a vision for lasting success. When leaders navigate tough decisions with empathy, transparency, and alignment with core values, they strengthen their leadership and create a culture of trust and accountability.

In the next chapter, we'll explore practical strategies for leadership in the digital age, where hybrid work environments and remote teams require new strategies for building connection and fostering collaboration.

PRACTICAL STRATEGIES FOR LEADING HYBRID TEAMS

Leading a hybrid team presents a unique set of challenges and opportunities that are distinct from leading an entirely in-office or remote workforce. Hybrid leadership requires a careful balance between flexibility and structure, where trust, accountability, and communication must be fostered across both physical and virtual boundaries.

In this chapter, we'll explore key strategies that will help you effectively lead a hybrid team. These strategies, grounded in Ethan's experience at Brightpath, can apply to any organization seeking to thrive in today's increasingly hybrid work environments.

1. ESTABLISH CLEAR COMMUNICATION CHANNELS

One of the most significant challenges of hybrid leadership is ensuring that communication flows freely and effectively between remote and in-office team members. Without clear, intentional communication strategies, remote employees can easily feel disconnected or overlooked.

A sample Hybrid Meeting Best Practices Checklist template is available in the tools and resources chapter at the end of this book.

Actionable Strategies:

- **Standardize Communication Tools:** Choose a central platform for team communication (e.g., Slack, Microsoft Teams) and ensure everyone—whether remote or in-office—uses the same tools consistently. This creates transparency and keeps everyone informed.

- **Create Structured Meeting Cadences:** Regular check-ins are essential to keep hybrid teams aligned. Schedule weekly virtual meetings for the entire team, regardless of location, to review progress, address concerns, and reinforce team cohesion.

- **Asynchronous Communication:** Encourage asynchronous communication for updates and progress tracking, especially when teams are working across multiple time zones. Tools like Trello, Notion, or Monday.com can help keep projects moving with no need for constant real-time communication.

- **Clear Meeting Agendas and Roles:** For every meeting, have a well-defined agenda and clear roles. Ensure that remote employees can speak and contribute. Avoid side conversations that exclude remote participants.

2. PROMOTE INCLUSIVITY AND EQUAL OPPORTUNITIES

A common pitfall of hybrid teams is the unintentional favoritism that arises when in-office employees get more face time with leadership, which can leave remote employees feeling marginalized. As a leader, it's crucial to create a fair situation for all employees, no matter their location.

Actionable Strategies:

- **Rotate Leadership Responsibilities:** Rotate meeting facilitators between in-office and remote team members. This gives everyone a chance to take on leadership roles and be visible across the organization.

- **Virtual Office Hours:** As a leader, hold regular virtual office hours that are open to remote employees. This ensures they have easy access to you and can address concerns or ideas without feeling distant.

- **Hybrid Mentorship Programs:** Pair remote and in-office employees together for mentorship opportunities. This not only helps remote workers feel more integrated into the company culture, but also promotes the exchange of ideas across different work environments.

- **Recognize Achievements Publicly:** Highlight the contributions of remote employees in company-wide meetings, newsletters, or intranet channels. Public recognition goes a long way toward fostering inclusivity and ensuring remote workers feel valued.

3. BUILD A CULTURE OF TRUST AND ACCOUNTABILITY

Trust is the foundation of any successful team, and in a hybrid environment, it becomes even more critical. Remote employees need to feel trusted to do their jobs without being micromanaged, while in-office employees need to trust that their remote counterparts are doing their share of the work.

Actionable Strategies:

- **Results-Driven Accountability:** Focus on outcomes, not activity. Judge employee performance based on results and achievements rather than time spent in the office or online. This removes biases that may arise from physical presence and ensures that both remote and in-office employees are held to the same standards.

- **Trust Through Transparency:** Encourage open and honest communication between team members about workloads, deadlines, and project statuses. When employees feel trusted to manage their time and tasks, they are more likely to take ownership of their work.

- **Set Clear Expectations:** For remote employees, clarity is key. Be clear about what's expected, when it's due, and how often the team should communicate. When expectations are transparent, remote workers are more empowered to meet them without constant oversight.

- **Encourage Flexibility with Accountability:** Allow employees flexibility in their work schedules, particularly remote workers who may need to manage different time zones or personal obligations. Set clear deadlines and hold them accountable for their contributions.

4. FOSTER TEAM CONNECTION AND CULTURE

One of the biggest challenges in a hybrid team is building a strong sense of connection among employees who may rarely, if ever, see each other in person. Without deliberate efforts to foster team bonding and culture, remote employees can feel isolated, and team dynamics can suffer.

Actionable Strategies:

- **Video On:** Encouraging team members to keep their cameras on during video calls is a simple yet powerful way to foster connection and engagement in hybrid teams. When participants can see each other's faces, it creates a more personal and collaborative atmosphere, helping to bridge the gap between remote and in-office employees. Facial expressions and body language—critical elements of communication—can be conveyed on video, so in-person and remote staff can exchange ideas and build rapport, reducing the likelihood of misunderstandings.

- **Virtual Team-Building Activities:** Organize regular virtual team-building exercises that include everyone. These can range from online games to problem-solving challenges, and they can help foster a sense of camaraderie across the team. Tools like Kahoot, Jackbox Games, or virtual escape rooms are great for this purpose.

- **Hybrid Social Hours:** Set up virtual social hours where the team can gather informally. For example, you can host a monthly "coffee chat" or "happy hour" over a video call where employees can discuss non-work-related topics.

- **Company-Wide Initiatives:** Foster a unified company culture by creating initiatives that engage both remote and in-office employees. For example, a company-wide challenge, such as a wellness program, can bring everyone together regardless of location.

- **Periodic In-Person Gatherings:** If workable, plan occasional in-person team gatherings that allow both remote and in-office employees to meet face-to-face. This helps strengthen relationships that are primarily built online.

5. LEVERAGE TECHNOLOGY FOR EFFECTIVE COLLABORATION

Hybrid teams rely heavily on technology to bridge the physical gap between remote and in-office employees. However, leaders must ensure effective use of the right tools to enhance collaboration—simply having them isn't enough.

Actionable Strategies:

- **Invest in Collaboration Tools:** Equip your team with the best collaboration tools, such as shared document platforms (Microsoft 365, Google Workspace, etc.), project management software (Asana, Microsoft Project, etc.), and video-conferencing tools (Zoom, Microsoft Teams, etc.). Train both remote and in-office employees on how to use these tools effectively.

- **Leverage Cloud-Based Systems:** Ensure that all documents, files, and resources are cloud-based so that employees can access them from anywhere at any time. This eliminates the friction that comes with working across different locations and time zones.

- **Hybrid Meeting Rooms:** If your company uses physical meeting rooms, consider setting them up as hybrid meeting rooms equipped with high-quality video and audio technology. This ensures that remote employees can fully take part in meetings as though they were in the room.

- **Optimize for Time Zones:** Be mindful of time zone differences when scheduling meetings or deadlines. Use tools like Microsoft Outlook or World Time Buddy to find overlapping hours that work for everyone and be flexible when remote employees need to work outside traditional hours. If there is a regular meeting and you cannot find a time that works for everyone who needs to be there, make sure you rotate the burden of meeting outside of standard working hours between all the meeting attendees. This will prevent the perception that those in the same time zone as the company's main office receive preferential treatment.

CONCLUSION: LEADING IN A HYBRID WORLD

Leading a hybrid team requires more than just adapting to different locations—it requires rethinking how leadership works. Ethan's experiences at Brightpath taught him that successful hybrid leadership relies on trust, inclusivity, and a strong culture that bridges both the virtual and physical worlds.

By implementing these practical strategies—establishing clear communication, promoting inclusivity, building trust, fostering team connection, and leveraging technology—you can create a hybrid team that thrives. Hybrid leadership is not just about managing the present—it's about shaping the future of work.

CONCLUSION

YOUR LEADERSHIP JOURNEY

Leadership is an ongoing journey—a process of continuous growth, reflection, and adaptation. Throughout this book, we've explored key leadership principles that not only build high-performing teams, but also foster trust, accountability, and innovation. From servant leadership to navigating crises, from fostering a culture of innovation to leading in the digital age, you've learned how each of these principles contributes to a more effective, empathetic, and impactful leadership style.

As you move forward in your own leadership journey, it's important to remember that leadership is about more than just results. It's about **how** you achieve those results—by empowering your team, maintaining integrity, and creating a culture where people feel valued and motivated to do their best work.

SUMMARY OF KEY LEADERSHIP PRINCIPLES

Let's take a moment to recap the core leadership principles we've covered in Part Two:

1. Trust as the Foundation of Leadership

Trust is the cornerstone of any successful leader's tool kit. It fosters open communication, collaboration, and accountability. Without trust, no team can function effectively. As a leader, you must work consistently to build and maintain trust with your team by being transparent, consistent, and empathetic.

2. Transparent Communication

Open and honest communication is key to building trust and fostering a culture of accountability. Leaders who communicate clearly and transparently create an environment where their teams feel informed, respected, and empowered to take ownership of their work.

3. Accountability Built on Trust

Trust, not fear, builds true accountability. Leaders must create systems of accountability that encourage personal ownership and align with the team's goals and values. This allows for a culture where everyone feels responsible for the success of the organization.

4. Servant Leadership

Servant leaders put the needs of their team first, fostering trust, loyalty, and long-term success. By focusing on serving others, leaders create an environment where team members feel valued, supported, and empowered to perform at their best.

5. Leading Through Crisis

Leadership is profoundly tested during crises. How you lead through uncertainty—by staying calm, communicating transparently, and maintaining accountability—will define how your team emerges on the other side. Crises are opportunities for leaders to show integrity, build trust, and strengthen the team.

6. Fostering Innovation

Innovation requires a culture that encourages risk-taking, creativity, and collaboration. Leaders who encourage their teams to try new things by prioritizing curiosity and continuous learning help their teams to be creative and solve hard problems.

7. Navigating Difficult Decisions

Leadership often involves making tough decisions that impact the future of the team or organization. By aligning these decisions with core values, being transparent about your choices, and owning the outcome, you build credibility and trust, even in challenging moments.

8. Leadership in the Digital Age

Leading in a hybrid or remote work environment requires new strategies to maintain connection, trust, and collaboration. Leaders must leverage technology, embrace flexibility, and foster a sense of community across dispersed teams to drive success in the digital era.

FINAL CALL TO ACTION: LEAD WITH PURPOSE AND INTEGRITY

Now that you've explored these key leadership principles, it's time to take action. Leadership is not just about knowing the right strategies—it's about applying them in your day-to-day management responsibilities. Whether you're leading a small team or an entire organization, the way you lead matters. It's the difference between building a culture of trust, accountability, and innovation and creating an environment where people feel disconnected and disengaged.

As you continue your leadership journey, remember that growth never stops. There will always be new challenges, new opportunities, and new lessons to learn. Seize each day as an opportunity to hone your leadership skills, empower your team, and make a lasting impact.

REFLECTION EXERCISE: ASSESS YOUR LEADERSHIP DEVELOPMENT

To help you reflect on your own leadership journey and set goals for the future, here are some prompts and questions to guide your thinking:

1. Building Trust

- How do I currently build trust with my team?

- Are there areas where I can be more transparent in my communication and actions?

- What can I do to strengthen the trust my team has in me and each other?

- How consistent am I in my actions, and do they align with the values I promote to my team?

2. Fostering Accountability

- How do I hold myself and my team accountable for our actions and results?

- Are my systems of accountability empowering, or do they create fear?

- How can I create a culture where accountability is embraced as a shared responsibility?

3. Serving Others

- Am I serving my team in a way that fosters growth and empowerment?

- What can I do to better understand the needs, concerns, and aspirations of my team members?

- How can I incorporate more servant leadership principles into my daily leadership approach?

4. Navigating Crisis

- How have I handled crises in the past?

- What lessons have I learned from leading through uncertainty?

- How can I better prepare myself and my team for future challenges?

5. Encouraging Innovation

- Do I create an environment where my team feels safe to innovate and take risks?

- How can I encourage more creative problem-solving and experimentation within my team?

- What resources or support can I provide to foster greater innovation?

6. Leading in the Digital Age

- How well am I adapting to the challenges of leading in a hybrid or remote work environment?

- What tools or strategies can I implement to improve communication and connection with my remote or dispersed team members?

- How can I foster a sense of community and belonging within my team, even when we're not all in the same location?

7. Personal Growth and Leadership Development

- What are my leadership strengths, and how can I build on them?

- What areas of my leadership responsibilities need improvement, and what steps can I take to grow?

- What goals can I set for myself to become a more effective, empathetic, and inspiring leader?

YOUR LEADERSHIP JOURNEY CONTINUES

Leadership is not a destination—it's a journey. As you reflect on the lessons and strategies in this book, think about how you can apply them to your unique leadership context. Imagine fifteen years have gone by since Ethan took over as CEO at Brightpath, and he is preparing to retire. As he sits down with the next CEO to pass the torch, what wisdom would he share? We can be certain he would reflect on the core leadership principles that guided his journey and the collective effort of a capable, thoughtful team. A good leader leaves a legacy not just in results but in the values and culture they instill. If we assume that Ethan has succeeded, the company will have grown—expanding into new markets, adopting innovative technologies, and redefining its potential. Yet, its success will not be measured solely by growth, but by its steadfast commitment to the values that built it. In the real world, companies that thrive understand this balance: they evolve without losing sight of what truly matters. As leaders, our greatest achievement is to build something that endures beyond our tenure, rooted in principles that inspire future generations.

Your journey is and always will be a work in progress. Continue to learn, grow, and lead with purpose.

TOOLS AND RESOURCES

To download PDF copies of the resources in this section, visit our website at:

WWW.APEXCONSULTING.PARTNERS/TOOLS-AND-RESOURCES

or scan the following QR code:

As leaders, building a culture of trust, accountability, and collaboration is essential, especially in a hybrid environment. This section provides practical tools and resources to support you on this journey. Each tool helps you implement the principles covered in this book, whether you're leading a team in person, remotely, or across multiple time zones.

1. TRUST-BUILDING ASSESSMENT WORKSHEET

- **Purpose:** Evaluate your current behaviors and identify areas to build or reinforce trust with your team.

- **How to Use:** Reflect on questions such as:

  » How do I currently build trust with my team?

  » Are there areas where I can improve transparency or consistency?

  » How can I show my team that I trust them to make decisions aligned with our values?

- **Goal:** Develop an action plan for reinforcing trust and creating a foundation for open, honest communication.

2. ACCOUNTABILITY MATRIX

- **Purpose:** Clearly define responsibilities and expectations for each team member.

- **How to Use:** Create a matrix that outlines:

  » Each team member's core responsibilities.

  » Expected outcomes and performance metrics.

  » Regular check-in points to provide feedback and support.

- **Goal:** Foster a culture of accountability where each team member understands their role and is motivated to deliver their best.

3. HYBRID MEETING GUIDELINES

- **Purpose:** Improve engagement and productivity in hybrid meetings. Make sure you post these guidelines on your intranet and leave laminated copies in your conference rooms.

- **How to Use:** Before each meeting, consider:
    - » Assigning a rotating team member to lead.
    - » Setting a clear agenda with expected outcomes.
    - » Encouraging participation by assigning specific roles (e.g., timekeeper, note-taker).
    - » Ensuring each participant has an equal voice, whether remote or in-office.

- **Goal:** Conduct effective meetings that keep all team members connected and involved.

4. 360-DEGREE FEEDBACK TEMPLATE

- **Purpose:** Collect insights from peers, managers, and direct reports to gain a well-rounded view of performance.

- **How to Use:** Use this feedback form to evaluate strengths, areas for improvement, and alignment with company values. Ensure feedback is constructive and focused on growth.

- **Goal:** Provide balanced feedback that helps individuals understand their impact and encourages continuous improvement.

5. WEEKLY TEAM REFLECTION PROMPTS

- **Purpose:** Facilitate open discussions that reinforce trust and accountability within the team.

- **How to Use:** At the end of each week, set aside time for the team to reflect on prompts like:

  » What went well this week, and what could we improve?

  » Are there any challenges affecting our productivity or morale?

  » How can we support each other better in the week ahead?

- **Goal:** Create a safe space for exchanging honest feedback and ensure the team remains aligned on goals and values.

6. RESOURCE LIST FOR CONTINUOUS LEARNING

- **Books:**

  » *The Speed of Trust* by Stephen M.R. Covey—A guide on how trust impacts success in business.

  » *Leaders Eat Last* by Simon Sinek—Insights on building trust within teams.

- **Podcasts:**

  » *The Modern Leadership Podcast*—Covers leadership, culture, and teamwork strategies.

- **Webinars and Courses:**

    » LinkedIn Learning's "Building a Culture of Trust"—Provides strategies for establishing trust in teams.

    » Coursera's "Managing Hybrid Teams"—Practical advice for leading hybrid teams.

These tools and resources serve as practical extensions of the leadership principles covered in this book. Remember, effective leadership is an ongoing journey of growth and adaptation. Use these resources as a foundation, but be open to refining your approach as your team and environment evolve.

ACKNOWLEDGMENTS

No journey is ever completed alone, and I have been fortunate to have had the support, guidance, and encouragement of incredible people throughout my career and the creation of this book.

First and foremost, I want to thank **Christy Paskevich** and **Vera Pavlicek**, who were at BioMarin when I first joined. Christy and Vera took a chance on me, welcoming me into their team and giving me the opportunity to grow both professionally and personally. Their belief in me from the start laid the foundation for everything I've achieved since.

I am equally grateful to **Mark Wood**, who served as the Head of HR when I began at BioMarin. Mark's support during my time there and his continued mentorship long after have been invaluable to my career. His guidance has been a constant source of wisdom and perspective.

A special thank you to **Rich Ranieri**, Head of HR after Mark Wood left BioMarin, for offering me the opportunity to take part in a rotational program. That experience gave me a more well-rounded perspective and played a critical role in shaping my career path.

To **Susan Hanan**, my boss when I joined Zogenix, I extend my deepest gratitude. Susan trusted me and provided me with the opportunity to manage IT, helping me step into a new leadership role and develop skills that have stayed with me ever since.

To **John Godbout**, who served as the Head of Global Talent at BioMarin, thank you for pushing me into challenging situations. Your support, even in the most difficult moments, helped me grow in ways I couldn't have imagined.

I also appreciate the incredible teams I've had the privilege of leading and working alongside over the years—your dedication, talent, and resilience have been a constant source of inspiration. Leadership is nothing without the teams who make it possible, and I am grateful for the lessons I've learned from each of you along the way.

I want to express my heartfelt appreciation to **Emma Knapper**, my girlfriend and partner. Emma, your adventurous spirit and unwavering support through all my crazy ideas and endeavors have been a source of strength and inspiration. You have been with me every step of the way, and I couldn't have done this without you.

A very special thank you to my parents: My mom, **Pat Williams**, and my dad and stepmom, **Rick and Ruth Peterson**, as well as my extended family, for pushing me out of my comfort zone but making sure I always had plenty of unconditional love. Your belief in me has been a driving force throughout my life, and I am forever grateful for your constant support.

A huge thank you to my editors, **Ania Erdogan**, **Susan Hanan**, **Christy Paskevich**, **Emma Knapper**, **Jessica Schmidt**, and especially **Art Kleiner**. You helped grow this book from good to great!

You have each left an indelible mark on my journey, and your influence is scattered throughout this book's pages. Thank you for everything.

ABOUT THE AUTHOR

Mike Peterson is a dynamic and accomplished executive with over fifteen years of experience in human resources and information technology, leading global initiatives across North America, Europe, and Asia. Having practiced HR in seventeen countries and traveled to every state in the US, Mike has developed a unique perspective: leadership principles are universal, provided they are applied with cultural sensitivity and flexibility.

As the Founder and Managing Partner of Apex Consulting Partners LLC, Mike specializes in solving complex business challenges by integrating innovative people strategies with cutting-edge technology solutions. Throughout his career, Mike has held global positions at BioMarin Pharmaceutical Inc., Zogenix Inc., UCB, and Structure Therapeutics, where he spearheaded transformational changes that improved employee engagement, streamlined processes, and enhanced organizational performance. He's an expert in HR, with experience in talent acquisition, performance management, workforce analytics, and diversity, equity, and inclusion (DEI) initiatives, making him a versatile leader in HR strategy.

With a strong background in IT operations, infrastructure, and cybersecurity, Mike has led high-impact projects that optimized enterprise applications, enhanced digital collaboration, and strengthened cybersecurity practices. He is known for aligning technology with business strategy, ensuring organizations are both efficient and secure. Mike's ability to bridge the gap between technical innovation and people-first leadership has earned him recognition as a trusted adviser and change agent in both HR and IT domains.

Mike holds a Bachelor of Science degree in Health and Exercise Science from Colorado State University and has been a certified professional through the Society of Human Resources Management (SHRM-CP) and the HR Certification Institute (PHR).

At the core of Mike's leadership philosophy is the belief that trust, accountability, and servant leadership are the cornerstones of building high-performing teams. He has helped organizations navigate change, foster innovation, and create cultures where people thrive. By balancing people-first leadership with technological advancement, Mike continues to drive organizations toward sustainable success.

In addition to his professional accomplishments, Mike is passionate about mountain biking and traveling with his partner, Emma, his two dogs, Spark and Zion, and his cat, Bolt. An avid adventurer, Mike never misses an opportunity to explore new landscape, new cultures, or new cuisines. Whether biking through rugged mountain trails, immersing himself in the energy of a bustling city, or tackling complex business challenges, he approaches every journey with curiosity and resilience.

With a career marked by innovation and leadership, Mike continues to influence the intersection of HR and IT, driving organizations toward sustainable success.

ABOUT APEX CONSULTING PARTNERS

This book addresses leadership challenges with broad application from the vantage point of the skills and insights developed at our firm, Apex Consulting Partners. Every leadership challenge is unique—just like every organization, department, or team. That's why one-size-fits-all approaches often fall short, no matter the size or scope of the organization. At Apex Consulting Partners, we specialize in crafting tailored strategies that unlock the best solutions for your specific needs, whether you're facing complex challenges or want to elevate your team's performance to the next level.

Our expertise spans organizations of all sizes. We are committed to helping you lead with clarity, purpose, and confidence. By partnering with Apex, you'll gain access to actionable insights and proven methodologies designed to foster a culture of trust, accountability, and sustainable success.

No matter the scale of your challenge, we're here to help. Visit us at https://www.apexconsulting.partners/ to learn more about our consulting services and discover how we can help your organization thrive.

www.ingramcontent.com/pod-product-compliance
Lightning Source LLC
Chambersburg PA
CBHW030451100526
44580CB00005B/74/J